Employment Law

Fourth Edition

Cavendish
Publishing
Limited

London • Sydney • Portland, Oregon

Fourth edition first published in Great Britain 2004 by
Cavendish Publishing Limited, The Glass House,
Wharton Street, London WC1X 9PX, United Kingdom
Telephone: + 44 (0)20 7278 8000   Facsimile: + 44 (0)20 7278 8080
Email: info@cavendishpublishing.com
Website: www.cavendishpublishing.com

Published in the United States by Cavendish Publishing
c/o International Specialized Book Services,
5824 NE Hassalo Street, Portland,
Oregon 97213-3644, USA

Published in Australia by Cavendish Publishing (Australia) Pty Ltd
45 Beach Street, Coogee, NSW 2034, Australia

Cataloguing in Publication Data
Data available

ISBN 1-85941-876-7

1 3 5 7 9 10 8 6 4 2

Typeset by Phoenix Photosetting, Chatham, Kent
Printed and bound in Great Britain

Contents

1 The contract of employment

Employed or self-employed?

The difference between an employee and a self-employed person is of crucial importance for a number of reasons. Only employees qualify for:

- ⮕ Social Security payments, such as jobseeker's allowance, statutory sick pay, etc;
- ⮕ employment protection rights, such as unfair dismissal, redundancy payments, minimum notice on termination, etc. Rights under the Sex Discrimination Act 1975; the Race Relations Act 1976; Pt II of the Employment Rights Act (ERA) 1996 (unlawful deductions from wages); and the Disability Discrimination Act 1995 are the significant exceptions – their coverage extends beyond employees to independent contractors who personally perform the task. Generally speaking, EC law applies to 'workers', a broader term than 'employees';
- ⮕ certain health and safety provisions;
- ⮕ the benefit of the employer's duty of care at common law (see *Lane v Shire Roofing Co (Oxford) Ltd* (1995));
- ⮕ taxation under Schedule E to the Income and Corporation Taxes Act 1988, and tax is deducted under the PAYE system, whereas a self-employed person is liable to tax under Schedule D, with its more generous allowances.

The terminology is as follows: an employee is employed under a contract of employment (or of service), whereas a self-employed person works under a contract for services.

A statutory definition

Section s 230(1) of the ERA 1996 defines an employee as 'an individual who has entered into or works under a contract of service'. This definition is not particularly helpful. One has to look at the case law for guidance.

Statutory interpretation by case law

A number of tests have emerged over a period of time:

- the 'control' test: *Yewens v Nokes* (1880), applied in *Walker v Crystal Palace Football Club* (1910);
- the 'integration' test: *Stevenson, Jordan and Harrison v MacDonald and Evans* (1952);
- the 'multiple', 'economic reality' or 'entrepreneurial' test: *Ready Mixed Concrete v Ministry of Pensions* (1968); followed by the 'business' test in *Market Investigations v Ministry of Social Security* (1969); in cases such as *Hall (HM Inspector of Taxes) v Lorimer* (1994) the courts have taken a more overall or 'holistic' view of the situation, and warned against the strict application of tests.

Sources and terms of the contract of employment

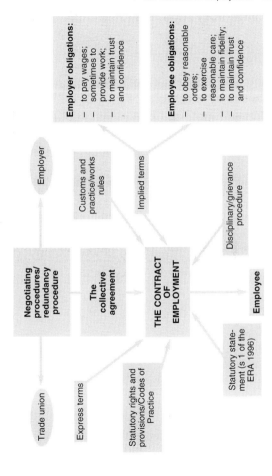

Employer obligations:
– to pay wages;
– sometimes to provide work;
– to maintain trust and confidence

Employee obligations:
– to obey reasonable orders;
– to exercise reasonable care;
– to maintain fidelity;
– to maintain trust and confidence

Employer

Customs and practice/works rules

Implied terms

Negotiating procedures/redundancy procedure

The collective agreement

THE CONTRACT OF EMPLOYMENT

Disciplinary/grievance procedure

Trade union

Express terms

Statutory rights and provisions/Codes of Practice

Statutory statement (s 1 of the ERA 1996)

Employee

In determining employment status, the modern approach has been to adopt a multi-factorial test, weighing up the various factors for and against the existence of a contract of employment. *Ready Mixed Concrete v Ministry of Pensions* (1968) lays down a three stage test (which has been impliedly approved by the House of Lords in *Carmichael v National Power* (2000)):

- the worker agrees to provide his work in return for a wage;
- the worker agrees to be subject to the control of the other party; and
- the other provisions of the contract are consistent with it being a contract of employment.

Carmichael v National Power (2000) states that there must be mutuality of obligation between the parties, as evidenced by the existence of a contract, and there must exist a sufficiency of control by the 'employer' over the worker – only if both of these conditions are satisfied should a court go on to find that a contract of employment exists (see *O'Kelly and Others v Trusthouse Forte* (1983)).

In the case of work which is part time, casual or otherwise 'atypical', the case law is at times confusing. The current position is best defined by *Carmichael v National Power plc* (2000) (HL), as applied in such cases as *Montgomery v Johnson Underwood Ltd* (2001) – whether there is mutuality of obligation and a sufficiency of control between the parties is a question of fact for the tribunal.

While there is no checklist of factors and the significance of each factor varies from case to case, a term in the contract that the worker need not personally do the job is a strong indicator that he is self-employed: *Express and Echo Publications Ltd v Tanton* (1999). See also *MacFarlane v Glasgow CC* (2001).

A question of law or fact?

Whether a contract is a contract of employment or a contract
for services has now been clearly stated to be a question of
fact, unless the sole issue is the construction of documents.
As such, it is a matter for the employment tribunal, as long as
it directs itself properly as to the legal tests to be applied (see
McLeod v Hellyer Bros Ltd (1987); *Lee v Chung and Shun
Sing Construction & Engineering Co Ltd* (1990); cf *Davies v
Presbyterian Church of Wales* (1986)).

Self-description

The fact that the parties have labelled the relationship as one
of self-employment is not viewed as a decisive factor by the
courts; it is merely one factor to be considered (see *Ferguson
v John Dawson & Partners Ltd* (1976); *Young and Woods Ltd
v West* (1980); *Lane v Shire Roofing Co (Oxford) Ltd* (1995);
cf *Massey v Crown Life Insurance Co* (1978)).

The individual contract and its sources

Features:

- inequality of bargaining power;
- informality.

Sources:

- express terms;
- collective bargaining;
- implied terms;
- work rules;
- custom and practice;
- statute;
- awards under statutory provisions.

Statutory rights, particularly those which arise on the termination of the contract, have largely replaced contractual terms, but those rights are founded on the 'cornerstone' of contract. For this reason, among others, contract law remains important.

All the normal contractual rules, such as offer, acceptance, consideration and legality, apply to the contract of employment.

Only in exceptional cases must the contract itself be in writing, for example, cases involving the Merchant Shipping Act 1995 and contracts of apprenticeship. Covenants in restraint of trade are examples of express terms.

Written particulars

Most employees possess the right to receive a written statement of some of the most important terms not later than two months after entering employment (see s 1 of the ERA 1996). Changes must be notified to employees individually, at the latest, not more than one month after the change.

The statement may be given in instalments during the two month period (s 1 of the ERA 1996). However, certain particulars must be contained in a single document. These are the names of the parties; the dates when employment and continuous employment commenced; the particulars of remuneration; hours and holidays; the job title or description; and the place of work (s 2(4) of the ERA 1996).

Particulars which must be supplied

The written statement must specify:

- the names of the employer and the employee;
- the date that the employment began;
- the date that the employee's period of continuous employment began (taking into account any employment

with a previous employer which counts towards that period);

- the scale or rate of remuneration, or the method of calculating remuneration;
- the intervals at which remuneration is paid;
- any terms and conditions relating to hours of work (including any terms and conditions relating to normal working hours);
- any terms and conditions relating to:
  - entitlement to holidays, including public holidays and holiday pay;
  - incapacity to work due to sickness or injury, including any provisions for sick pay;
  - pension and pension schemes;
- the length of notice which the employee is obliged to give and entitled to receive in order to terminate the contract of employment;
- the title of the job which the employee is employed to do or a brief description of the work for which the employee is employed;
- where the employment is not intended to be permanent, the period for which it is expected to continue or, if it is for a fixed term, the date on which it is to end;
- either the place of work or, if the employee is required or permitted to work at various places, an indication of that and the employer's address;
- any collective agreements which directly affect the terms and conditions of employment, including the persons by whom they were made where the employer is not a party;
- where the employee is required to work outside the UK for more than a month, certain further particulars concerning that period, the currency of remuneration, any additional remuneration and benefits, and any terms and conditions relating to return.

Prior to the Trade Union Reform and Employment Rights Act (TURERA) 1993, not all of the information had to be given directly in written form. Following the coming into force of the Act, the law has been tightened up in a number of ways (see ss 1–12 of the ERA 1996).

The statement is not a contract in itself

Until 1982, it was thought that s 1 statements had virtually equivalent weight to a written contract, that is, they were affected by the parol evidence rule (see *Gascol Conversions v Mercer* (1974)).

However, since *System Floors v Daniel* (1982), the position is as follows:

> It seems to us ... that, in general, the status of the statutory statement is this. It provides very strong *prima facie* evidence of what were the terms of the contract between the parties, but does not constitute a written contract between the parties. Nor are the statements of the terms finally conclusive: at most, they place a heavy burden on the employer to show that the actual terms of contract are different from those which he has set out in the statutory statement.

Remedies for failure to supply

See ss 11–12 of the ERA 1996 and *Eagland v British Telecom* (1992). See also *Mears v Safecar Security Ltd* (1982) and *Construction Industry Training Board v Leighton* (1978).

The products of collective bargaining

Collective agreements between employers and trade unions are not binding on those parties, but terms of the agreements may be incorporated into individual contracts of employment and so become legally binding between employers and their employees.

Effects of the collective bargaining on the individual contract of employment

There are three possible methods of incorporation:

- agency;
- express incorporation; and
- implied incorporation.

Agency

See *Holland v London Society of Compositors* (1924); *Burton Group Ltd v Smith* (1977); cf *Singh v British Steel Corp* (1974); *Land v West Yorkshire MCC* (1979).

Express incorporation

There are three problems:

- What is the effect on the terms of an individual contract when an incorporated agreement is cancelled? See *Robertson v British Gas Corp* (1983); *Gibbons v Associated British Ports* (1985); cf *Cadoux v Central Regional Council* (1986); *Davies v Hotpoint Ltd* (1994).
- Is the legal status of the source of the incorporated term important? See *Marley v Forward Trust Group* (1986).
- The appropriateness question: see *Gallagher v Post Office* (1970); *BL v McQuilken* (1978); *Alexander v Standard Telephone and Cables Ltd* (1991); *City of Edinburgh Council v Brown* (1999). A pay increase is the obvious example of a term which is suitable for incorporation into an individual employment contract.

Implied terms

Despite the increasing role played by statute (for example an equality clause imposed into all contracts of employment by the Equal Pay Act 1970), common law implied terms are still

9

of considerable importance. New terms can still be 'discovered'.

The traditional test for implication is subjective and the courts will imply a term:

> ... of which it can be predicated that it goes without saying; some term not expressed but necessary to give to the transaction such business efficacy as the parties must have intended [*Luxor Ltd v Cooper* (1941), *per* Lord Wright].

Is this test based on industrial reality?

There are two distinctive types of terms:

- those implied due to the particular circumstances of the case, often known as terms implied in fact;
- those implied due to the operation of the common law, often known as terms implied in law.

Factual implied terms

These terms are inserted into the contract of employment through the normal contractual tests, such as the business efficacy and 'officious bystander' tests. It was once thought that the correct approach was that of the usual subjective rules, but an approach which comes nearer to that of implying terms where they would be reasonable has been adopted: see *Mears v Safecar Security Ltd* (1982); *Jones v Associated Tunnelling Co Ltd* (1981); *Courtaulds Northern Spinning Ltd v Sibson* (1988); *Eagland v BT plc* (1992). However, cf *Quinn v Calder Industrial Materials Ltd* (1996).

Terms implied by common law

Although many of these have evolved from the 19th century, there is no reason to suppose that this is a static area of law.

There are generally thought to be the following implied duties on the part of the employer:

- to pay wages;
- (sometimes) to provide work;
- to exercise care;
- to co-operate.

The employee's duties

The duties of the employee are generally thought to be:

- to obey reasonable orders;
- to exercise reasonable care and competence;
- to maintain fidelity;
- to be honest;
- not to compete;
- not to misuse confidential information;
- not to impede the employer's business;
- to account.

The employer's duties

A right to work?

In general, the employer will not be in breach of contract by failing to provide work, as long as wages continue to be paid:

> ... Provided I pay my cook her wages regularly, she cannot complain if I choose to take any or all of my meals out [*Collier v Sunday Referee Publishing Co Ltd* (1940), *per* Asquith J].

Exceptions

There are exceptions to this general rule, including the following:

- where work depends wholly or partially on piecework payment or commission (see *Turner v Goldsmith* (1891));
- where part of the consideration is publicity, for example, where an actor needs publicity in order to acquire his

next role (see *Herbert Clayton and Jack Waller Ltd v Oliver* (1930));

⮕ where skills need to be maintained (see *Breach v Epsylon Industries Ltd* (1976)).

See also *Langston v AUEW* (1974).

To exercise care

Employers are under a threefold duty, namely, to provide a safe place of work, safe equipment and safe colleagues: *Wilsons & Clyde Coal Co Ltd v English* (1938). For an interesting development, see *Johnstone v Bloomsbury HA* (1991); *Cross v Highlands Enterprise* (2001); *Spring v Guardian Assurance plc* (1993).

Mutual trust and confidence

See *Isle of Wight Tourist Board v Coombes* (1976); *Woods v WM Car Services* (1981); *Lewis v Motorworld Garages* (1986); *Malik v Bank of Credit and Commerce International* (1997).

The employee's obligations

Obedience to reasonable orders

With changing social attitudes, many of the earlier decisions upholding the employer's right to summarily dismiss employees for one act of disobedience would probably not be decided the same way today. See:

⮕ *Laws v London Chronicle Ltd* (1959);
⮕ *Wilson v Racher* (1974).

Unreasonable orders

The following have been held to be unreasonable orders:

- ⊃ ordering an employee into immediate danger (*Ottoman Bank v Chakarian* (1930));
- ⊃ ordering an employee to commit an illegal act (*Morrish v Henlys (Folkestone) Ltd* (1973)).

To what extent can an obligation to adapt to new techniques or other working conditions be read into the contract of employment?

See *Cresswell v IRB* (1984), *Hollister v NFU* (1979). If the change involves altering the contractual terms, the employer can only lawfully introduce change if either:

- ⊃ there is a term in the contract authorising fundamental variation; or
- ⊃ the employee has agreed to the change: cf *Burdett-Coutts v Hertfordshire CC* (1984); *Rigby v Ferodo* (1987); *Security and Facilities v Hayes* (2001).

Fidelity

This duty extends to obligations not to accept bribes, take secret profits or maintain the secrecy of one's colleagues' misdeeds, but it is in respect of competition that this duty is most often seen.

Competition whilst in employment

See, in particular:

- ⊃ *Hivac Ltd v Park Royal Scientific Instruments Ltd* (1946);
- ⊃ *Smith v DuPont (UK) Ltd* (1976);
- ⊃ *Nova Plastics Ltd v Froggatt* (1982).

Competition: ex-employees

An ex-employee is generally free to go into competition with his former employer. This is subject to two exceptions.

An employee may not do anything while still employed which is in breach of the duty of fidelity

See, for example, *Wessex Dairies Ltd v Smith* (1935); *Robb v Green* (1895); *Roger Bullivant Ltd v Ellis* (1987).

However, it is perfectly lawful for an ex-employee to canvass customers of his former employer after leaving his service. Moreover, he is entitled to make use of the knowledge and skills which he acquired whilst in his former employer's business, apart from such information which can be classified as trade secrets. In this sense, the implied duty of confidentiality for ex-employees is narrower than in the case of an existing employee: see *Faccenda Chicken Ltd v Fowler* (1986).

The Court of Appeal in that case provided guidelines on whether any item of information falls within the implied term of confidentiality, so as to prevent its use or disclosure by an employee after employment has ceased. The court will consider:

- the nature of the employment;
- the nature of the information, that is, is it a trade secret or some other highly confidential data?;
- whether the employer impressed on the employee the confidentiality of the information;
- whether the relevant information can be isolated from other information which the employee is free to use or disclose.

See also *Lancashire Fires Ltd v FA Lyons* (1997); *SBJ Stevenson Ltd v Mandy* (2000).

There is a defence of 'just cause or excuse' to an employee's disclosure of confidential information.

The insertion of a restraint of trade clause

The second exception to an ex-employee's freedom to go into competition with his former employer may be the insertion of a restraint of trade clause in the contract of employment.

Only such interests as trade secrets, the stability of the workforce and customer connections may be protected by such a clause. Also, the restrictive covenant must be shown to go no further – in terms of scope, time and area of the restraint – than is reasonable, and it must generally be in the public interest: see *Littlewoods Organisation Ltd v Harris* (1978); *Greer v Sketchley Ltd* (1979). The courts will not generally re-write clauses which offend against the above, and any clauses which are ambiguous will be subject to the *contra proferentem* rule – it will be interpreted strictly against the party seeking to rely upon it. Wrongful dismissal invalidates an otherwise enforceable covenant: *Rock Refrigeration Ltd v Jones* (1996).

'Garden leave': some recent developments

See, particularly:

- *Evening Standard Ltd v Henderson* (1987);
- *Rex Stewart Ltd v Parker* (1988);
- *Provincial Financial Group plc v Hayward* (1989).

A garden leave clause will not be necessary where the employers have a contractual right to prevent the employee from coming into work and they are not under a duty to provide work: *William Hill Organisation Ltd v Tucker* (1999).

Impeding the employer's business

See *Secretary of State for Employment v ASLEF (No 2)* (1972) and *British Telecommunications plc v Ticehurst* (1992).

A 'new' implied term: the employer's obligation to bring contingent rights to the attention of employees

See *Scally v Southern Health and Social Services Board* (1991).

Work rules

See *ASLEF (No 2)*, above; *Dryden v Glasgow Health Authority* (1992).

Custom and practice

For custom to have a legal effect, it must be reasonable, certain and notorious. Does the worker have to be aware of the custom? See *Sagar v Ridenhalgh & Son* (1931); cf *Meek v Port of London Authority* (1918); *Quinn v Calder Industrial Materials Ltd* (1996).

Statute

See statutory implied terms giving rights: guaranteed pay, equal pay and minimum notice. Also, see the law on working time, which, in general, imposes a ceiling of 48 hours on working time per week. There are exceptions. The National Minimum Wage Act 1998 overrides arrangements to pay less than the minimum.

Also, on occasion, statute will render a contractual term void (s 203 of the ERA 1996).

Note that there are special rules governing the payment of wages (Pt II of the ERA 1996).

2 Equal pay

The main sources of law relating to equality between men and women in terms of pay are:

- Equal Pay Act (EPA) 1970;
- Art 141 of the EC Treaty;
- Directive 75/117, the Equal Pay Directive.

Inequality in pay which is based on race is governed by the Race Relations Act 1976: *Wakeman v Quick Corp* (1999).

European Community law

Article 141 of the Treaty establishes the principle of equal pay for equal work. The Article is directly enforceable in the Member States and takes precedence over domestic law. It has to be read subject to Directive 75/117, the Equal Pay Directive, which fleshes it out. Whilst the Directive is not directly enforceable against individual employers, Art 141 must be interpreted in accordance with it; consequently it is, in effect, applied directly.

The meaning of 'pay'

'Pay' means ordinary, basic or minimum wage or salary and any other consideration in cash or kind.

'Equal pay' means for the 'same work or for work to which equal value is attributed' (Art 1).

Article 141 is directly enforceable in the national courts: *Jenkins v Kingsgate (Clothing Productions) Ltd* (1981).

The EPA 1970 must be interpreted in the light of Art 141 to ensure consistency of approach: *Pickstone v Freemans plc* (1989). If, however, domestic law provides an adequate remedy, then EC law will not be directly enforceable by the complainant: *Blaik v Post Office* (1994).

The meaning of the word 'pay' in EC law has been interpreted in a flexible way, providing additional scope to the domestic legislative provisions. For example, 'pay' may include:

- benefits paid under a contracted out occupational pension scheme (*Barber v Guardian Royal Exchange Assurance Group* (1991));
- sick pay (*Rinner-Kühn v FWW Spezial-Gebäudereinigung GmbH* (1989));
- concessionary rail travel (*Garland v British Rail Engineering Ltd* (1982));
- piecework schemes (*Specialarbejderforbundet i Danmark v Dansk Industrie (acting for Copenhagen A/S)* (1995));
- compensation for unfair dismissal (*R v Secretary of State for Employment ex p Seymour-Smith* (1999)).

Equal Pay Act 1970

This implies an equality clause into every contract of employment. The equality clause will operate to equalise pay related terms in a contract of employment where there is a man and woman employed on:

- like work;
- work rated equivalent;
- work of equal value.

The meaning of 'pay' within the EPA 1970

Each term of the remuneration package should be considered individually and should be equalised (*Hayward v Cammell*

Laird Shipbuilders (1988)), even though this may give rise to 'leap-frogging'.

Occupational benefits fall within the meaning of the word 'pay' (*Griffin v London Pension Fund Authority* (1993)); redundancy and *ex gratia* payments are also included (*McKechnie v UBM Building Supplies (Southern) Ltd* (1991)).

The comparator

Any claim must be brought by a member of the opposite sex (there is no 'class action', as exists in the USA) who is employed in the same employment as the comparator, that is, either by the same employer or an associated employer, and either at the same establishment or at an establishment where common terms and conditions are observed (s 1(6) of the EPA 1970):

- 'employed' means employed either under a contract of service or a contract personally to execute work or labour. If this is the major obligation under the contract, then the contract falls within the EPA 1970 (*Mirror Group Newspapers Ltd v Gunning* (1986));
- 'common terms and conditions' means terms and conditions which are substantially comparable on a broad basis. It is, therefore, sufficient for the applicant to show that his comparators at another establishment or at his establishment were employed on broadly similar terms (*British Coal Corp v Smith* (1996));
- Art 141 extends the range of comparators to those employed in the same establishment or service (*Scullard v Knowles* (1996)), but cannot be used to compare completely different organisations (*Lawrence v Regent Office Care Ltd* (1999); *Allenby v Accrington & Rossendale College* (2001)); however, be aware of *South Ayrshire Council v Morton* (2002);

○ multi-comparators are allowed (*Langley v Beecham Proprietories* (1985));

○ predecessors may be comparators (*Macarthys Ltd v Smith* (1981)). Comparison with a successor is also permitted (*Diocese of Hallam Trustees v Connaughton* (1996));

○ an order for discovery may be obtained in order to identify the most appropriate comparator (*Leverton v Clwyd CC* (1989)); however, this may not be used as the right to undertake a 'fishing trip' to identify possible claims.

The heads of claim

Like work

The applicant must show that he is employed on 'like work' with his comparator (s 1(2)(a) of the EPA 1970). The work should, therefore, be the same or of a broadly similar nature. Differences which are not of practical importance can actually be disregarded. This allows the adoption of a 'broad brush' approach. For example, in *Electrolux Ltd v Hutchinson* (1977), male employees were paid a higher piecework rate for doing work of a broadly similar nature to female employees. However, the men could be asked to do more demanding work, to work nights and to do non-production work. The issue was whether these extra duties justified a higher rate of pay. The Employment Appeal Tribunal (EAT) concluded that they did not. The frequency with which they were asked to undertake this extra work was relevant, and this would have to be very frequent if the difference in pay was to be justified.

The following may be relevant:

○ additional responsibility may justify a difference in pay (*Eaton Ltd v Nuttall* (1977));

- the tribunal must consider what actually happens in practice, rather than what is contained in the job description (*Shields v E Coomes (Holdings) Ltd* (1978));
- the time at which work is carried out is not normally relevant, unless it brings with it additional responsibilities (*Dugdale v Kraft Foods Ltd* (1977); *Thomas v National Coal Board* (1987));
- where an applicant is employed on work of a higher value than that of the comparator, terms should be equalised, but he is not entitled to a higher wage (*Murphy v Bord Telecom Eireann* (1988)).

Work rated equivalent

This head of claim is dependent upon the employer having carried out a job evaluation scheme. If the scheme is an analytical scheme, in which the woman's work and the man's work have been rated as equivalent, then pay and other contractual terms must be the same (s 1(2)(b) of the EPA 1970). If the conclusion is to the contrary, then an applicant will not succeed in his or her claim for either 'like work' or 'work of equal value'. However, if the job evaluation scheme was not analytical or was discriminatory, an equal value claim may succeed. An analytical scheme should consider all matters connected with the nature of the work, including effort, skills and responsibilities: *Eaton Ltd v Nuttall* (1977). Analytical schemes include: *points assessment*, which breaks down each job into a number of factors, points being awarded for each factor on a pre-determined scale; and *factor comparison*, in which the evaluation is based on a limited number of factors, such as skills and responsibilities.

Non-analytical schemes include: *job ranking*, in which a ranking table of jobs is produced and the ranked jobs are grouped into grades; and *paired comparison*, in which one job is compared to another and, thereby, awarded points.

In addition, schemes may contain discriminatory job factors, such as dexterity or strength, which would allow the job evaluation scheme to be challenged under both the EPA 1970 and Directive 75/117 (*Rummler v Dato-Druck GmbH* (1987)).

If a company has a clear and non-discriminatory work evaluation scheme in place, this does of course provide the basis for a good defence to any claim for equal pay.

Work of equal value

The work of equal value provision allows the applicant to claim the same pay as her male comparator if she is doing work of the same value in terms of the demands made on her (s 1(2)(c) of the EPA 1970). Following the decision in *Pickstone v Freemans plc* (1988), an equal value claim may be made even though there is a man employed in the same job as the woman. This prevents an employer from using the 'token man' to block an equal value claim. However, where there is a genuine 'like work' claim, it is usually in the applicant's interest to pursue this course of action, as, in terms of procedure, such claims are less complicated than equal value claims.

Procedure for claims of equal value

Directions hearing

Initial hearing

Are there reasonable grounds for determining that the work is of equal value?

Consideration of the material factor defence

Should the claim be referred to an independent expert, or can the employment tribunal determine the outcome itself?

Reference to an independent expert

(where appropriate)

The independent expert will determine whether the work of the woman and the man is of equal value

Provide a date by which the independent expert will report to the employment tribunal

Following the independent expert's report, the hearing is resumed

What amounts to equal value?

The issue for the tribunal is whether to adopt a narrow or broad brush approach. For example, if the independent expert has reported that the applicant's job is valued at 97% of her comparator's job, is this work of equal value? If a broad brush approach is taken, it probably is. The current trend appears to be to adopt the broad brush approach: *Pickstone v Freemans plc* (1993).

Genuine material factor defence

The burden of proof is on the applicant to establish that her work falls within either the like work, work rated as equivalent or work of equal value provisions. Even where the applicant succeeds in this, the employer may still be able to avoid equalising terms by establishing the defence provided by s 1(3) of the EPA 1970. This defence allows the employer to prove that the variation in pay is genuinely due to a material factor other than sex. If the difference is not based on sex, no justification need be provided: *Strathclyde Regional Council v Wallace* (1998). The Equal Pay Act concerns equality of pay based on gender, not on fairness.

The s 1(3) defence may be raised at the preliminary hearing or at the full hearing, although it can no longer be pleaded at both.

What amounts to a 'genuine material factor/difference'?

The difference in pay must be objectively justified.

Red-circle agreements

These allow the employer to protect the salary of an employee or group of employees, even though he or they may have been moved to a lower grade of work: *Snoxell v Vauxhall Motors Ltd* (1977).

Different geographical areas

Different rates of pay or salaries may be justifiable for different locations: see *NAAFI v Varley* (1977).

Seniority: experience

This may justify a difference in pay, even though it might also discriminate against women whose careers may be interrupted due to care responsibilities: see *Nimz v Freie und Hansestadt Hamburg* (1991).

Skill and qualifications

See *Clay Cross (Quarry Services) Ltd v Fletcher* (1979).

Additional responsibility

Where the difference in pay is based on additional responsibilities, there must be actual and frequent tasks: *Shields v E Coomes (Holdings) Ltd* (1978).

Market forces

This may be an acceptable defence where there are genuine economic factors which affect, or have an impact upon, the employer's business: *Rainey v Greater Glasgow Health Board* (1987). However, the need to undertake compulsory competitive tendering is not an automatic defence: *Ratcliffe v North Yorkshire CC* (1995). Obviously, unlimited use of a market forces defence would totally undermine the effectiveness of the EPA – there will always, therefore, be a conflict between the purpose of the statute and market forces.

Collective bargaining and separate pay structures

These are not necessarily an automatic defence: *British Coal Corp v Smith* (1996); *Enderby v Frenchay HA* (1994). Following the decision in *Handels-og Kontorfunktionaerernes Forbund i Danmark v Dansk Arbejdsgiverforening (Acting for Danfoss)* (1989), it is clear that pay systems should be transparent so that it is clear to all parties why they are on a particular grade. In the absence of transparency, the burden of proof is on the employer to show that there is no discrimination. The mere existence of separate pay structures based on different collective agreements does not necessarily amount to objective justification: *British Road Services v Loughran* (1997).

An example of an employer failing in its defence is *North Yorkshire CC v Ratcliffe* (1995), where the House of Lords ruled that a variation in pay occasioned by compulsory competitive tendering was not justified.

Time limits and compensation

Limits imposed on claims for equal pay are as follows:

- compensation is limited to up to two years' back pay, unless the employer has concealed the difference in pay: *Levez v PH Jennings (Harlow Pools) Ltd* (1999). This limit is not to be applied if, by comparison with actions under similar national laws, claimants are disadvantaged: see *Levez v PH Jennings (Harlow Pools) Ltd (No 2)* (1999);

- the time limit for bringing claims is six months' employment preceding the date of reference to the employment tribunal. In *Preston v Wolverhampton Health Care NHS Trust* (1998), the House of Lords referred to the European Court of Justice the issue of whether this time limit was compatible with EC law. Following a ruling by the ECJ (*Preston v Wolverhampton Health Care NHS Trust* (2001)), the House of Lords held that it may be.

3 Discrimination

The main sources of law relating to discrimination are:

- Sex Discrimination Act (SDA) 1975;
- Race Relations Act (RRA) 1976;
- Disability Discrimination Act (DDA) 1995;
- Directive 76/207, the Equal Treatment Directive, which deals with sex discrimination only.

These laws can be seen as forming part of human rights law.

European Community law

EC law has had a significant impact in the field of discrimination, through Directive 76/207. This Directive can be enforced directly in the UK national courts against the State or an organ of the State as an employer, but not against a private employer: see *Foster v British Gas plc* (1991), in which an 'organ or emanation of the State' was held to include a body which has been made responsible for providing a public service under the control of the State and has, for that purpose, special powers beyond those which result from the normal rules applicable in relations between private individuals. One significant change resulting from the application of Directive 76/207 has been the equalisation of retirement ages for men and women: *Marshall v Southampton and South West Hampshire AHA (Teaching)* (1986). Although EC law has provided flexibility and additional scope in interpreting UK law, it does not extend to positive discrimination: *Kalanke v Freie und Hansestadt Bremen* (1995), where a preference for a female candidate, all other things being equal, was unlawful. However, a preference for a female in a job where women are underrepresented is lawful if the individual circumstances of the male applicant can be taken into account: *Marschall v Land Nordrhein Westfalen* (1998). By virtue of the Treaty of Amsterdam 1997, the EC has competence in the field of race discrimination.

UK law

Discrimination is unlawful if it is based on:

- race, colour, nationality, ethnic origin or national origin (ss 1 and 3 of the RRA 1976);
- sex (ss 1 and 2 of the SDA 1975);
- marital status (ss 1 and 3 of the SDA 1975);
- disability (s 1 of the DDA 1995).

It is important to remember that in UK law, case law under the RRA and SDA is generally interchangeable.

Racial grounds and racial groups

In order to bring a case under the RRA 1976, the complainant must show either that he has been discriminated against on racial grounds (direct discrimination) or that he belongs to a racial group and has, therefore, been subjected to indirect discrimination. This can be a contentious issue where there is a fine dividing line between race and religion; the latter was not covered by the RRA, but discrimination in employment on the grounds of religion or belief is now unlawful under the Employment Equality (Religion or Belief) Regulations 2003 (SI 2003/1660).

In *Seide v Gillette Industries Ltd* (1980), one of the issues was whether discriminating against a Jew amounted to religious discrimination or whether 'Jew' included a person of a particular race or ethnic origin. It was held that the word 'Jew' could mean any of these things and that the court had to look at why the person was being discriminated against. See also *Simon v Brimham Associates* (1987).

The test for determining racial group within s 3 of the RRA 1976 was provided in *Mandla v Dowell Lee* (1983). In this case, the words 'ethnic origin' were held to mean a distinct and separate community by reason of various characteristics, including: culture; language; history; descent; literature; religion; and any racial characteristics. As a result, a Sikh boy was held to be a member of a racial group. This test has been applied in the following cases: *CRE v Dutton* (1989) (gypsies); *Crown Suppliers v Dawkins* (1993) (rastafarians). 'National origins' are ascertained as identifiable elements, both historically and geographically, which reveal the existence of a nation: *Northern Joint Police Board v Power* (1997). For this reason, the Scots and the English have different *national* origins; therefore, it is unlawful for Scottish employers to discriminate against English job applicants. However, the Scots and the English do not have different *ethnic* origins because each group consists of people of many different ethnic origins (see *BBC Scotland v Souster* (2001)).

Sex

This term covered transsexuals (SDA amended by S1 1999/1102) but, according to the ECJ in *Grant v South West Trains Ltd* (1999), not homosexuals. See also *MacDonald v Advocate General for Scotland* (2003) (HL). In line with European requirements, the SDA has been amended by SI 2003/1661 to include discrimination on the grounds of sexual orientation.

Marital status

The SDA 1975 prohibits discrimination on the grounds of marriage but does not render unlawful discrimination against single persons.

Disability

The DDA 1995 does not apply to employers employing fewer than 15 employees. Section 1 of the DDA 1995 and the Discrimination (Meaning of Disability) Regulations 1996 define 'disability' as the following:

- a physical or mental impairment which has an adverse effect on his ability to carry out normal day to day activities: *Law Hospital NHS Trust v Rush* (2001);
- the effect is substantial: *Foster v Hampshire Fire and Rescue Service* (1998);
- the effect is long term.

Types of discrimination

Burden of proof and the need for a comparator

Following the Sex Discrimination (Indirect Discrimination and Burden of Proof) Regulations 2001, it is no longer necessary for the complainant to prove their case, merely to establish the facts of the complaint. The onus then moves to the employer to provide an acceptable explanation which is not based on unlawful discrimination. However, discrimination should be inferred from the facts where the employer cannot offer a satisfactory explanation.

Finally, both the SDA 1975 (s 5) and the RRA 1976 (s 3) impose a statutory, 'like with like' comparison: *Bain v Bowles*

(1991). However, such a comparison is not required under the DDA 1995 (*British Sugar plc v Kirker* (1998)). In relation to discrimination against pregnant women, no male comparator is used. The same is true of sexual harassment: *British Telecommunications plc v Williams* (1997). Dress codes are a problematic area of law.

Direct discrimination

The concept of direct discrimination is aimed at preventing overt and covert discrimination of the individual. It is a concept common to sex, race and disability discrimination. The following must be established:

- a woman (or man), disabled person or member of a racial group has been treated less favourably than a man (or woman), able-bodied person or person of a different race;
- the reason for the treatment is based on the person's sex, disability or race;
- the test for establishing direct discrimination, laid down in *R v Birmingham CC ex p EOC* (1989) and confirmed in *James v Eastleigh BC* (1990):
  - was there an act of discrimination?;
  - but for the applicant's *sex, disability or race,* would he or she have been treated differently (that is, more favourably)?

If both questions are answered in the affirmative, direct discrimination is established. Motive is irrelevant: *Grieg v Community Industry* (1979). The conduct of the hypothetical employer is not the basis of the test for direct discrimination: *Zafar v Glasgow CC* (1998). Therefore, the 'range of reasonable responses' test used in unfair dismissal is not applicable in discrimination cases.

The RRA also provides for *transferred* discrimination. This means that discrimination may take place when a person is treated less favourably because of another person's race. For example, in *Showboat Entertainment Centre Ltd v Owens* (1984), Owens, who was white, was dismissed from his job as the manager of an amusement centre for failing to obey an order to exclude black people. Unlawful discrimination was held to have taken place. See also *Weatherfield Ltd t/a Van and Truck Rentals v Sargent* (1998).

The DDA 1995 provides for the justification of the act of discrimination on the part of the employer if it is 'material' to the circumstances and is a 'substantial' reason, for example, where the disability prevents the person from performing his job.

Section 6 of the DDA imposes a duty on employers to make reasonable adjustments to their premises and the ways in which they operate in order to accommodate disabled employees and applicants. This duty only applies where:

- the employer knew or would reasonably be expected to have known of the disability (*O'Neill v Symm & Co* (1998) – but see *HJ Heinz Co Ltd v Kenrick* (2002));
- the applicant or employee is likely to be put at a substantial disadvantage by the existing premises or arrangements: *Ridout v TC Group* (1998).

Sexual and racial harassment

As there are no specific provisions relating to sexual harassment, it falls to be considered under the remit of direct discrimination. Racial harassment is now covered by SI 2003/1626.

A single act of a serious nature will support a claim of harassment: *Bracebridge Engineering Ltd v Darby* (1990). A single verbal comment, if sufficiently serious, may amount to harassment: *In Situ Cleaning v Heads* (1995).

Racial insults may amount to harassment, but it must be shown that they were directed towards the complainant or were reasonably likely to have an effect on his feelings, so that a detriment has been suffered: *De Souza v Automobile Association* (1986). Note, however, that the harassment itself is normally accepted to amount to a detriment.

The complainant must also show that he has suffered a detriment when claiming sexual harassment. This may have an impact on the amount of compensation awarded: *Snowball v Gardener Merchant Ltd* (1987); *Wileman v Minilec Engineering Ltd* (1988).

Employers are vicariously liable for discriminatory acts – including harassment – carried out by their employees, unless the employer can show that he took all reasonable steps to prevent the occurrence of the act (s 32 of the RRA 1976; s 41 of the SDA 1975; s 58 of the DDA 1995). The test for vicarious liability is generally somewhat stricter than the common law test: *Tower Boot Co Ltd v Jones* (1997). This is to prevent the employer from successfully claiming that the employee was acting outside the course of his employment (the 'We don't pay him to do that' argument) when he carried out the act. For example, in *Tower Boot*, the complainant had been subjected to racist name calling, branding with a hot screwdriver and whipping. The Court of Appeal held that to allow the employer to succeed in his claim that the employees were acting outside the course of their employment would allow an employer to escape liability and lead to an increase in acts of harassment.

Employers will not be vicariously liable for actions of third parties (*MacDonald v Advocate General for Scotland* (2003) (HL), disapproving *Burton v De Vere Hotels* (1996)). See the Race Relations (Amendment) Act 2000, which extends the 1976 Act to functions of public authorities not previously covered, and which formally makes Chief Constables vicariously liable for acts of discrimination carried out by their police officers.

Further protection from sexual harassment is provided by the adoption of Recommendation 92/C27/04 on the protection of the dignity of men and women at work, which led to the publication of a Code of Practice on sexual harassment. Whilst the recommendation and the Code are not binding, following the decision in *Grimaldi v Fonds des Maladies Professionelles* (1990), national courts must take such non-binding measures into account in clarifying the interpretation of other provisions of EC and national law. It would, therefore, be expected that employers have adopted the Code of Practice: *Wadman v Carpenter Farrer Partnership* (1993).

Intentional harassment is now a criminal offence: s 4A of the Criminal Justice and Public Order Act 1994.

The Protection from Harassment Act 1997 allows the complainant to bring a civil action against the harasser. Harassment, in this case, is defined as being a course of conduct which amounts to harassment of another and which the perpetrator knows, or ought to know, amounts to harassment. There must have been at least two instances of harassment, although verbal harassment is included. Damages and/or an injunction may be awarded.

Segregation

This is a form of direct race discrimination. For segregation to amount to unlawful discrimination, there must be evidence that the segregation has arisen because of some policy on the part of the employer: *Pel Ltd v Modgill* (1980).

Pregnancy

To discriminate against a woman on the grounds of her pregnancy amounts to unlawful discrimination within both the SDA 1976 and Directive 76/207. The case law upholds the view that there is no need for the pregnant woman to compare herself with a hypothetical sick man: *Dekker v Stichting*

Vormingscentrum voor Jong Volwassenen (VJV – Centrum) Plus (1992); *Webb v EMO Air Cargo (UK) Ltd (No 2)* (1995), although the latter case suggests that this is restricted to non-fixed term contracts, whilst *Caruana v Manchester Airport plc* (1996) and the ECJ in *Jimenez Melgar* (2001) suggest that it applies equally to fixed term contracts.

It should be noted that:

- comparison with the sick man may, however, be appropriate once the maternity leave period is complete (*Handels-og Kontorfunktionaerernes Forbund i Danmark (acting for Hertz) v Dansk Arbejdsgiverforening (acting for Aldi Marked K/S)* (1991));

- protection for the pregnant woman ceases at the end of the maternity leave period (*British Telecommunications plc v Roberts and Longstaffe* (1996); *Handels-og Kontorfunktionaerernes Forbund i Danmark v Dansk Handel and Service (acting on behalf of Fotex Supermarked A/S)* (1997));

- dismissal of a woman whilst she is pregnant, on account of unfitness for work caused by the pregnancy, may constitute direct discrimination contrary to Art 5(1) of Directive 76/207 (*Brown v Rentokil Initial UK Ltd* (1998)).

Dismissal of pregnant women is automatically unfair under the ERA 1996.

Indirect discrimination

Indirect discrimination is aimed at conduct or practice which, on the surface, appears to be neutral or innocuous, rather than discriminatory, but which, in effect, has an adverse or disparaging impact on a particular sex or race. It should be noted that the concept of indirect discrimination is not found in disability discrimination.

The key elements in establishing discrimination under s 1(1)(b) of the SDA 1975 and s 1(1)(b) of the RRA 1976 are described below.

Requirement or condition imposed on all applicants

The burden of proof is on the complainant to establish that there is a requirement or condition. It was thought that a requirement or condition must be an essential criterion for the job: *Perera v Civil Service Commission (No 2)* (1983). However, following the decision of the EAT sitting in Scotland in *Falkirk Council v Whyte* (1997), criteria which are strongly desirable may also amount to requirements or conditions. Nevertheless, the EAT sitting in England held that it was bound by *Perera (No 2)* in *Coker v Lord Chancellor* (1999).

The following are examples of requirements or conditions:

- an age range (*Price v Civil Service Commission* (1978));
- a full time post (*Home Office v Holmes* (1985));
- a mobility clause (*Meade-Hill and National Union of Civil and Public Servants v British Council* (1995));
- a language qualification (*Perera v Civil Service Commission* (1983));
- a rule that the person appointed to be special adviser to the Lord Chancellor must be known to him (*Coker v Lord Chancellor* (1999));
- insistence on working from an office (*Lockwood v Crawley Warren Group Ltd* (2001)).

A 'considerably smaller proportion'

The next stage is for the complainant to establish that, in applying the requirement or condition, there has been an adverse impact on his sex or race. He must select the appropriate pool for comparison, supported by statistical evidence. The appropriate pool for comparison would normally be all those with the required qualifications for the post, not including the requirement complained of: *University of Manchester v Jones* (1993). At this stage, the 'like with like' comparison is relevant.

The template for establishing disparate impact, using sex discrimination against women as an example, is as follows:

- ⟳ take the number of women in the pool (of applicants for a job or promotion, for example);
- ⟳ take the number of women in the pool who can meet the requirement or condition;
- ⟳ divide (b) by (a) to give the proportion of women in the pool who can satisfy the requirement or condition;
- ⟳ the same calculation should now be done for men and a comparison made.

The employment tribunal may also have regard to the actual number of men/women employed. For example, if there are a small number of female employees in comparison to male employees, and only a small percentage can comply with the requirement or condition, this may still amount to a considerably smaller proportion: *London Underground Ltd v Edwards (No 2)* (1998); *Chief Constable of Avon v Chew* (2002).

Can comply

The complainant must then show that a considerably smaller proportion of women/his racial group 'can comply' with the requirement or condition compared to men or other persons.

The relevant date is the date that the discriminatory conduct operated: *Clarke v Ely (IMI) Kynoch Ltd* (1982).

'Can comply' means can comply in practice: *Price v Civil Service Commission* (1978). Women can physically comply with a rule that they must be aged between 17 and 28 to apply for a job but, in practice, fewer of them can apply than men because a higher percentage of women will be out of the labour market through having and rearing children.

Detriment

The complainant must then show that the requirement or condition is to his detriment. Detriment includes transferring a person to a less interesting post.

This provides the complainant with *locus standi* and establishes that a loss has been incurred: *Home Office v Holmes* (1985).

Justification

The onus now moves to the employer to show that the requirement or condition is justifiable, irrespective of the sex or race of the person to whom it is applied. Generalisations will not succeed.

The test of justifiability requires an objective balance between the discriminatory effect of the condition and the reasonable needs of the party who applies the condition: *Hampson v Department of Education and Science* (1989). The condition must be necessary and appropriate.

Victimisation

Both s 4 of the SDA 1975 and s 2 of the RRA 1976 make unlawful victimisation by employers of those employees who have either brought proceedings under the respective statutes or who have given evidence in proceedings taken against the employer: *Aziz v Trinity Street Taxis Ltd* (1988). The rule against victimisation applies both during and after employment: *Coote v Granada Hospitality Ltd* (1998). Therefore, references provided by ex-employers may be discriminatory: *Chief Constable of West Yorkshire Police v Khan* (2001).

Employment

The complainant must establish that he has been discriminated against, either in respect of employment (s 6 of the SDA 1975; s 4 of the RRA 1976; s 4 of the DDA 1995) or in relation to the provision of goods, facilities and services, education, etc. In the employment field, this covers the arrangements for selection for employment (for example, when a job offer is withdrawn when the employers discover that the employee-to-be is pregnant), terms on which employment is offered, or the refusal or omission to offer employment. It also covers discrimination during the employment relationship, that is, access or refusal of access to opportunities for promotion, transfer or training, as well as the termination of employment or subjecting the complainant to any other detriment. 'Detriment' amounts to any conduct which would result in the reasonable worker taking the view that he had been disadvantaged in the circumstances in which he had to work: *De Souza v Automobile Association* (1986); *Gary v London Borough of Ealing* (2001).

Genuine occupational qualifications

These provide the employer with a possible defence if he can show that sex or race is a genuine occupational qualification, for example, the necessity for women to model bikinis. The sex or race of the post holder must be a required attribute and not a sham: see *Tottenham Green Under Fives' Centre v Marshall (No 2)* (1991).

It is not a genuine occupational qualification to employ only women in a female dress shop (*Etam plc v Rowan*

(1989)) or only men in a men's clothing shop (*Wiley v Dee and Co (Menswear) Ltd* (1978)). If, at the time of the complaint, there are no employees because the business has not begun to operate, the genuine occupational qualification defence may still operate: *Lasertop Ltd v Webster* (1997).

Compensation

The principal remedy for discrimination is compensation, but tribunals may also make a declaration and issue a recommendation that the employer removes the discrimination. There is no statutory limit on the amount of compensation awarded (cf claims for unfair dismissal). Interest is payable on compensation: *Marshall v Southampton and South West Hampshire AHA (Teaching) (No 2)* (1994).

Note the following:

- all awards for compensation should include a sum for injury to feelings (*Sharifi v Strathclyde Regional Council* (1992); *Armitage, Marsden and HM Prison Service v Johnson* (1997); *O'Donoghue v Redcar Borough Council* (2001));
- claims for discrimination can include claims for damages for personal injury, including psychiatric harm (*Sheriff v Klyne Tugs (Lowestoft) Ltd* (1999); *HM Prison Service v Salmon* (2001));
- aggravated damages may be awarded (see *Alexander v Home Office* (1988)). Exemplary damages are not available in discrimination cases (*Ministry of Defence v Meredith* (1995));
- there is a three month time limit from the date of the last alleged act for bringing claims.

The Employment Relations Act 1999 and the Employment Act 2002

The Employment Relations Act introduced a right to unpaid leave for parents to care for children under five years born after 18 December 1999. It also provided a right to take unpaid leave to cope with domestic emergencies concerning dependants. The Employment Act 2002 provides for further maternity and paternity rights, including time off for adoptive parents.

4 Termination of employment

Terminations involving dismissal at common law

Dismissal with notice

The length of notice should be expressly agreed by the parties. If no notice is expressly agreed, then the common law requires that 'reasonable notice' should be given, with the length depending on such factors as the seniority and status of the employee. Apart from any contractual provision for notice, an employee is entitled to a statutory minimum period of notice. The employer must give one week's notice to an employee who has between one month and two years' service, and then not less than one week's notice for each further year of continuous service, up to a maximum of 12 years. In return, the employee must give at least one week's notice of resignation if employed for more than a month (s 86 of the ERA 1996).

Dismissal for breach of a fundamental term

The conduct of the employee may be viewed as being sufficiently serious to justify immediate termination of employment without notice. In this event, the employee will lose entitlement to both contractual and statutory minimum notice. Examples include wilful disobedience of a lawful order, theft of or wilful damage to the employer's property, violence at work, dishonesty, etc. An employer should make clear what it considers to amount to gross misconduct.

Wrongful dismissal

This is defined as dismissal with no or insufficient notice where the employers cannot justify their failure to give (sufficient) notice. The remedy is damages, which are assessed on contractual principles. For example, damages run only until the end of the notice period and the doctrine of mitigation applies. As far as remedies for dismissal are concerned, the following weaknesses have been identified:

- the low level of damages awarded to successful litigants, generally only compensating for the appropriate notice period which should have been given: see *Addis v Gramophone Co Ltd* (1909); *Bliss v SE Thames RHA* (1985). For example, damages cannot be awarded to compensate for the stress of losing a job, injured feelings or the manner of dismissal. More recently, however, the House of Lords has partly side-stepped the long established approach in *Addis*. In *Malik v BCCI SA (In Liq)* (1997), their Lordships allowed 'stigma' damages to be recovered by ex-employees of BCCI in respect of injury to their reputations allegedly caused by the bank conducting a dishonest and corrupt business – however, their Lordships made clear that the decision should be confined to the particular facts of the case; see *Johnson v Unisys Ltd* (1999);

- the lack of procedural protection for most employees, with only so called office holders and those whose employment has 'statutory underpinnings' being entitled to natural justice and the remedies of public law (see *Ridge v Baldwin* (1964)). More recent attempts to broaden the range of workers in the public sector who could apply for judicial review as an alternative remedy to unfair dismissal have been strongly resisted by the courts. It has been held that, where the dispute involves private rights arising out of the contract of employment, as opposed to public rights, then judicial review is inappropriate (see *R v Berkshire HA ex p Walsh* (1984));

🔁 the inability of dismissed employees to regain their jobs because of the general rule against ordering specific performance of contracts. More recently, this rule has been relaxed and injunctions restraining dismissals and breaches of contract by employers have been granted where the court has been satisfied that trust and confidence remained between the parties (see *Irani v South West Hampshire HA* (1985); *Powell v London Borough of Brent* (1987); *Hughes v London Borough of Southwark* (1988); *Boyo v Lambeth Borough Council* (1995); *Anderson v Pringle of Scotland Ltd* (1998)).

Once the quantum of damages has been assessed, various deductions are made, including deductions for redundancy payments and the compensatory award for unfair dismissal.

Terminations not involving dismissal at common law

Death or dissolution of the employer

But see below, p 50.

Frustration

'Frustration' is a legal concept which, if it applies, brings the employment contract automatically to an end, without resulting in a dismissal. As a result, there is no liability to continue paying wages or to pay compensation for unfair dismissal, redundancy, etc.

In order for the doctrine of frustration to apply, two essential factors must be present:

🔁 there must be some event, not foreseen or provided for by the parties to the contract at the time it was made, which either makes it impossible for the contract to be performed at all or at least renders its performance radically different from that which the parties envisaged when they made the contract; and

○ the event must have occurred without the fault of either contracting party. Frustration will not operate if it was 'self-induced' or caused by the fault of a party.

Events that have been held to frustrate the contract include:

○ the conscription of the employee to national service;
○ internment as an enemy alien during wartime.

However, frustration arguments have been most frequently employed in the case of long term absence through sickness or imprisonment.

Where absence is due to sickness, a number of factors will generally be relevant in deciding whether a contract is frustrated. These include:

○ the terms of the contract, including any provision for sick pay;
○ how long the employment would be likely to last in the absence of sickness;
○ whether the employee holds a 'key position';
○ the nature of the illness and how long it has already continued, and the prospects of recovery;
○ the period of past employment.

The leading cases from which this test is derived are: *Marshall v Harland and Wolff Ltd* (1972); *Egg Stores (Stamford Hill) Ltd v Leibovici* (1977); *Hart v AR Marshall & Sons (Bulwell) Ltd* (1977); and *Notcutt v Universal Equipment Co Ltd* (1986).

In *Williams v Watsons Luxury Coaches Ltd* (1990), Wood J warned against too 'easy' an application of the doctrine; otherwise, there would be no scope for the doctrine of dismissal, with the effect that no remedy could be awarded for wrongful dismissal, unfair dismissal or on redundancy.

In the past, imprisonment was thought to be 'self-induced' frustration. More recently, however, the Court of Appeal has ruled that a custodial sentence of six months does have the effect of frustrating the contract. It was felt that it was the sentence passed by the trial judge – as opposed to the employee's criminal conduct – which was the frustrating event. Consequently, this was not a case of self-induced frustration: *FC Shepherd & Co Ltd v Jerrom* (1986).

Expiry of a fixed term contract

The expiry of a fixed term contract does not constitute a dismissal at common law, but it is deemed to be a dismissal by statute (see below).

Termination by mutual agreement

As with other contracts, a contract of employment may be terminated by the mutual consent of the parties. If the courts were to accept too readily that the contractual relationship had ended in this way, then access to employment protection would be severely threatened. In general, courts and tribunals have been reluctant to accept the argument that an employee has, in reality, agreed to give up his job and to forgo the possibility of an unfair dismissal or redundancy claim. The general principle which the courts will apply is that, if the sole cause of the employee's willingness to agree to resign is the threat of dismissal, he will be taken to have been dismissed (see *Sheffield v Oxford Controls Ltd* (1979)). If, however, other additional factors, such as financial inducements, affected his decision, it will be held that there was termination by mutual agreement: *Logan Salton v Durham CC* (1989); *Birch v University of Liverpool* (1985). The question is: who really terminated the contract (*Martin v MBS Fastenings (Glynwed) Distribution Ltd* (1983))?

An agreement for the automatic termination of a contract of employment on the occurrence of a certain event may be void under s 203(1) of the ERA 1996 (*Igbo v Johnson Matthey Chemicals Ltd* (1986)).

Terminations deemed to be dismissals under the Employment Rights Act 1996

Death or dissolution of the employer

An act of the employer or any event affecting the employer (including death, dissolution of a partnership or winding up of a company) which has the effect of automatically terminating the contract at common law will be deemed to be dismissal for the purposes of redundancy, but not for an unfair dismissal claim: s 136(5) of the ERA 1996.

Termination of a contract by the employer with or without notice

See ss 95(1)(a) and 136(1)(a) of the ERA 1996.

Ambiguous/unambiguous words of dismissal/resignation

The legal principles in this area may be summarised as follows:

- if, taking into account the context in which they were uttered, the words unambiguously amount to a dismissal (or resignation), then this should be the finding of the tribunal (see *Sothern v Franks Charlesly & Co* (1981));
- where, however, the words employed are ambiguous because they were uttered in the heat of the moment, the

effect of the statement is determined by an objective test, that is, whether any 'reasonable' employer or employee might have understood the words to be tantamount to a dismissal or resignation (*BG Gale Ltd v Gilbert* (1978));

⮕ a dismissal or resignation given in the heat of the moment may generally be withdrawn. However, the change of mind must not be so late that it is impossible to recover the words' effect (*Martin v Yeoman Aggregates Ltd* (1983)), nor, presumably, must the words used etc be sufficient to breach mutual trust and confidence.

The Court of Appeal considered these principles in *Sovereign House Security Services Ltd v Savage* (1989). It confirmed that an employment tribunal is entitled to look behind what was said unambiguously and find that, in the context or circumstances (such as a decision taken in the heat of the moment or by an immature employee), there was no real termination, despite appearances (see also *Kwik-Fit v Lineham* (1992)).

Failure to renew a fixed term contract

See ss 95(1)(b) and 136(1)(b) of the ERA 1996.

The expiry of a fixed term contract is deemed by statute to be a dismissal. It must have a definite starting and finishing date, although there may be provision for earlier termination by notice within the fixed term period: *BBC v Dixon* (1979).

Following the Fixed Term Employees (Prevention of Less Favourable Treatment) Regulations 2002, where an employee has been continuously employed under fixed term contracts for more than four years, and where the use of such fixed term contracts could not be objectively justified, the employee is taken to be permanently employed.

Where an employee is employed on a fixed term contract for more than two years, it was in the past possible for such an employee to agree in writing to waive any right to a redundancy payment; however, following the Fixed Term Employees (Prevention of Less Favourable Treatment) Regulations 2002 (above) it is no longer possible for employers to require this of their employees.

Note the distinction between fixed term contracts, on the one hand, and contracts to perform specific tasks or terminable on the occurrence of a specific event, on the other. In the latter category of cases, it has been held that there is no dismissal when the task is completed or the contingent event occurs: *Brown v Knowsley BC* (1986). It should, however, also be noted that for the purpose of the Fixed Term Employees (Prevention of Less Favourable Treatment) Regulations 2002, both types of contract are taken to be 'fixed term contracts'.

Constructive dismissal

Where the employee terminates the contract, with or without notice, by reason of the employer's conduct, this will be 'constructive dismissal': ss 95(1)(c) and 136(1)(c) of the ERA 1996. The leading case is *Western Excavating v Sharp* (1978).

The elements of the concept are:

- Has the employer broken a term of the contract or made it clear that he does not intend to be bound by the contract?
- If yes, is the term which has or will be broken an essential or fundamental term of the contract?
- If yes, has the employee terminated the contract with or without notice in response to the breach within a reasonable time?

Constructive dismissal may occur if the employer breaks an express term of the contract, such as by reducing pay

(*Industrial Rubber Products v Gillon* (1977)) or failing to follow a prescribed disciplinary procedure (*Post Office v Strange* (1981)). It can also occur if there is a breach of an implied term, such as the duty to provide a reasonably suitable working environment (*Waltons and Morse v Dorrington* (1977)), the duty to provide access to a grievance procedure (*WA Goold (Pearmak) Ltd v McConnell and Another* (1995)) or the duty to maintain mutual trust and confidence. Some case illustrations of breaches of the latter term follow:

- failing to respond to an employee's complaints about the lack of adequate safety equipment (*British Aircraft Corp v Austin* (1978));
- failing to provide an employee with reasonable support to enable him to carry out his job without disruption and harassment from fellow employees (*Wigan BC v Davies* (1979));
- failing to properly investigate allegations of sexual harassment or to treat the complaint with sufficient seriousness (*Bracebridge Engineering Ltd v Darby* (1990));
- imposing a disciplinary penalty grossly out of proportion to the offence (*BBC v Beckett* (1983));
- a series of minor incidents of harassment over time which cumulatively amount to repudiation: the so called 'last straw doctrine' (*Woods v WM Car Services (Peterborough)* (1982)).

The implied duty of trust and confidence appears, at times, to override an employer's strict rights under the contract. In other words, employers must exercise their contractual powers in such a way as not to destroy trust and confidence: *United Bank Ltd v Akhtar* (1989); *White v Reflecting Roadstuds Ltd* (1991); *Bass Leisure v Thomas* (1994).

A constructive dismissal is not necessarily unfair: *Savoia v Chiltern Herb Farms Ltd* (1982).

5 Unfair dismissal

Employees have the (conditional) right not to be unfairly dismissed (s 94 ERA).

Unfair dismissal	➲ Time limit in which to lodge a claim is usually three months
	➲ Remedies – compensation, reinstatement or re-engagement
	➲ Limit on compensation
	➲ Forum – employment tribunal (EAT on appeal)
	➲ Proceedings – relatively informal
	➲ Employee must have been employed for qualifying period – currently one year – for the majority of dismissals
	➲ Employee must not have reached normal retiring age
	➲ Compensation can be reduced by up to 100% for contributory fault
	➲ Acts or omissions discovered after dismissal are not relevant to the fairness issue (though they could reduce compensation)
Wrongful dismissal	➲ Under the Statute of Limitation, the time limit is six years
	➲ Damages are the main remedy
	➲ No limit on compensation
	➲ Forum – county court or High Court (appeal to the Court of Appeal or, in Scotland, to the Court of Session). Since 1994, employment tribunals have had the jurisdiction to hear termination of contract claims of up to £25,000, with some exceptions, such as covenants in restraint of trade
	➲ Usual court rules and formalities apply
	➲ No qualifying period
	➲ No age limit
	➲ No account is taken of the employee's action contributing to dismissal
	➲ Acts or omissions discovered after dismissal will be taken into account

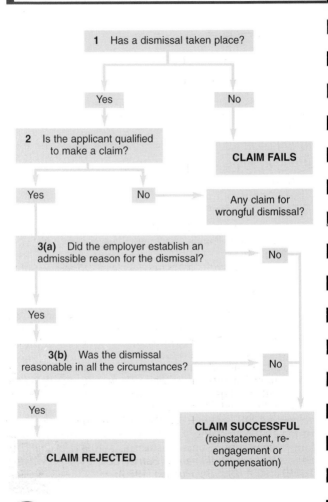

1 Has a dismissal taken place?

Yes → No

2 Is the applicant qualified to make a claim?

No → **CLAIM FAILS**

Yes → No → Any claim for wrongful dismissal?

3(a) Did the employer establish an admissible reason for the dismissal? → No

Yes

3(b) Was the dismissal reasonable in all the circumstances? → No

Yes

CLAIM SUCCESSFUL (reinstatement, re-engagement or compensation)

CLAIM REJECTED

Unfair dismissal

Stage 1: has a dismissal taken place?

The meaning of dismissal

This was discussed in Chapter 4. The term covers express dismissal, the expiry of a fixed term contract and constructive dismissal.

Stage 2: is the applicant qualified to make a claim?

There are three issues here:

- Is the applicant an 'employee'? (See Chapter 1)
- Does the applicant's employment fall within an excluded category?
- Has the applicant presented the claim in time?

Excluded categories

Much of the legislation concerning excluded categories has been repealed. The major remaining category is those employees who have reached retirement age. An employee may not normally complain of unfair dismissal if, on or before the effective date of termination, he has attained the age which, in the undertaking in which he was employed, is the normal retiring age for an employee holding the position which he held and the retiring age is the same for men and women: s 108(1) of the ERA 1996. Where there is no normal retiring age, employees aged 65 and over may not normally bring a complaint of unfair dismissal: s 109(1) of the ERA 1996. See also *Nothman v Barnet LBC* (1979), *Waite v GCHQ* (1983), *DHSS v Hughes* (1985).

In most cases, continuous employment for one calendar year is required in order to claim. It is therefore necessary to identify the effective date of termination (EDT) *see below*. A statutory definition of continuous employment is given in ss 210–13 ERA (see also *Ford v Warwickshire County Council* (1983); *Flack v Kodak Ltd* (1987); cf *Booth v USA* (1999)).

Strikes do not break continuity of employment but time on strike is not counted towards the one year qualifying period.

Other excluded categories include the following:

- Workers engaged in official action who, at the time of their dismissal, are taking industrial action or are locked out where there has been no selective dismissal or re-engagement of those taking the action. Unofficial strikers may be selectively dismissed or re-engaged (ss 237 and 238 of the Trade Union and Labour Relations (Consolidation) Act (TULR(C)A) 1992).
    - Those taking part in industrial action who are sacked within eight weeks of the start of the action are deemed to be unfairly dismissed. Protection extends beyond the eight week period if the employers have not taken reasonable steps to resolve the dispute (Employment Relations Act 1999).
- Illegal contracts: a contract of employment to do an unlawful act is unenforceable.
- Those employees covered by a disciplinary procedure, voluntarily agreed between employers and an independent trade union, where the Secretary of State has designated it to apply instead of the statutory scheme (s 110 of the ERA 1996).
- Where a settlement of the claim has been agreed with the involvement of an ACAS conciliation officer and the

employee has agreed to withdraw his complaint (s 203(2)(e) of the ERA 1996), and where the employee enters into a valid compromise contract satisfying the conditions set out in s 203(3). These include the condition that the employee should have taken independent legal advice.

Claim in time

In common with the enforcement of most other employment protection rights, an applicant must present a claim within three months of the effective date of termination. This time limit is fairly rigorously applied, although it confers upon employment tribunals a discretion to allow a claim to be presented within a reasonable time outside the three month period where it considers that it was not reasonably practicable for the complaint to be presented in time (s 111 of the ERA 1996).

The leading cases in this area state that the test to be applied in determining whether a late claim should be considered is not confined to whether the applicant knew of the right to claim, but extends to a consideration of whether he *should* have known: *Dedman v British Building and Engineering Appliances* (1974); *Walls Meat Co Ltd v Khan* (1987). Illness is an example of a valid reason for delay. Erroneous advice as to the time limits given to the applicant by a 'skilled adviser', such as a lawyer, trade union official or Citizens Advice Bureau worker, will not excuse a late application: *Riley v Tesco Stores Ltd* (1980) – any claim for negligent misstatement lies against the adviser. However, where the erroneous advice was given by an employment tribunal clerk, this does provide an excuse for a late claim: *Jean Sorelle Ltd v Rybak* (1991). The fact that the employee was pursuing an appeal through the employer's internal proceedings does not provide an excuse. It is a question of fact – as opposed to a question of law – whether it was 'reasonably practicable' to claim in time: *Palmer v Southend on Sea BC* (1984).

The effective date of termination (s 97)

The qualifying period is calculated up to and including the effective date of termination. The ERA 1996 offers a statutory definition of the date of termination for both unfair dismissal and redundancy payment claims and, although it is called the 'effective date of termination' for unfair dismissal purposes and the 'relevant date' for redundancy payments, the definition is largely the same in both cases. The effective date of termination is defined as follows:

- where the contract of employment is terminated by notice, whether by employer or employee, the date of termination is the date on which the notice expires (ss 97(1)(a) and 145(2)(a));
- where the contract of employment is terminated without notice, the date of termination is the date on which the termination takes effect (ss 97(1)(b) and 145(1)(b)). If an employee is summarily dismissed with wages in lieu of notice, the 'effective date of termination' is the actual date on which the employee is told of dismissal, and not the date on which the appropriate notice period would expire (*Robert Cort & Sons v Charman* (1981); *Stapp v Shaftesbury Society* (1982); *Batchelor v BRB* (1987));
- where the employee is employed under a contract for a fixed term, the date of termination is the date on which the term expires.

Stage 3: is the dismissal fair or unfair?

See s 98(4) of the ERA 1996.

Reason for the dismissal: potentially fair reasons

See s 98(1)–(2):

- capability or qualifications, such as illness;
- conduct, such as disobedience and theft;
- redundancy (see Chapter 6 for the definition);
- the employee could not continue to work without contravention of a statute, as occurs when a delivery driver loses his licence;
- some other substantial reason, such as when a customer exerts pressure on the employer to dismiss the employee or an employee refuses to accept new contractual terms of employment.

An employer will only be allowed to rely upon facts known at the time of the dismissal to establish what was the reason for the dismissal. Facts which come to light after the dismissal cannot be relied upon to justify the dismissal, though they may persuade a tribunal to reduce compensation: *W Devis & Sons Ltd v Atkins* (1977).

Dismissals which are deemed to be unfair

Certain reasons for dismissal are regarded as automatically unfair and do not require one year's continuous employment before claims may be made. These are as follows:

- dismissal for trade union membership and activity, where the union is independent, or for a refusal to join a trade union or particular trade union, whether the union is independent or not (s 152 of TULR(C)A 1992);

the transfer of an undertaking or as a 'protected' or 'opted out' shop or betting worker; or refused to work on a Sunday;

- dismissal on the grounds that the employee:
  - carried out, or proposed to carry out, duties as a safety representative or as a member of a safety committee;
  - where there was no representative or committee, or it was not reasonable to raise the matter with them, brought to the employer's attention, by reasonable means, harmful or potentially harmful circumstances;
  - left the place of work, or refused to return to it, in circumstances of danger which the employee reasonably believed to be serious or imminent and which he could not reasonably have been expected to avert; or
  - in circumstances of danger, took or proposed to take appropriate steps to protect himself or others from the danger (s 100 of the ERA 1996);

- dismissal where the employee brought proceedings against the employer to enforce a 'relevant statutory right' or alleged an infringement of such a right. 'Relevant statutory rights' are those conferred by the ERA 1996, for which the remedy is by way of complaint to an employment tribunal; notice rights under s 86 of the ERA; and rights relating to deductions from pay, union activities and time off under TULR(C)A 1992;

- dismissal of an employee who is a trustee of an occupational pension scheme established under a trust if the reason (or, if more than one, the principal reason) for the dismissal is that the employee performed (or proposed to perform) any of the functions of a trustee (s 102 of the ERA 1996);

- dismissal for taking part in industrial action within eight weeks of the start of the strike or within a longer period if the employers do not take reasonable steps to resolve the dispute (Employment Relations Act 1999);
- dismissal of a woman because she is pregnant, for a reason connected with her pregnancy or childbirth or for making use of maternity laws (s 99 of the ERA 1996);
- dismissal because of a conviction which is spent under the terms of the Rehabilitation of Offenders Act 1974 (s 4(3)(b));
- dismissal connected with the transfer of an undertaking, unless there are economic, technical or organisational reasons entailing changes in the workforce (see reg 8 of the Transfer of Undertakings (Protection of Employment) Regulations 1981 (SI 1981/1794));
- dismissal on the ground of redundancy if the circumstances constituting the redundancy also applied equally to one or more employees in the same undertaking who held posts similar to that held by the dismissed employee and who have not been dismissed and:
  - the reason (or, if more than one, the principal reason) for selecting the employee for dismissal was union related (s 153 of TULR(C)A 1992); or
  - the reason for selection was because of pregnancy or childbirth or because the employee had: been involved in raising or taking action on health and safety issues; asserted certain statutory rights (see below); performed (or proposed to perform) any functions as a trustee of an occupational pension scheme; performed (or proposed to perform) the functions or activities of an employee representative for the purpose of consultation over redundancies or

- dismissal of a 'protected' or 'opted out' shop or betting worker for refusing to work on a Sunday or for giving (or proposing to give) an opting out notice to the employer (s 101 of the ERA 1996). Broadly, shop or betting workers are 'protected' if, before the commencement dates of the legislation which liberalised Sunday trading and betting, they were not required under their contract of employment to work on Sunday. Shop or betting workers who are contractually required to work on Sunday may give three months' written notice of their intention to 'opt out' of Sunday working at the end of the notice period, but not before (Pt IV of the ERA 1996);

- dismissal for making a protected public interest disclosure (s 103A of the ERA 1996); for the meaning of 'protected disclosure', see Pt IVA of the ERA 1996: both of these provisions were inserted by the Public Interest Disclosure Act 1998.

The reasonableness of the dismissal

If the dismissal is not deemed to be unfair ('automatically unfair'), the tribunal considers its fairness. See s 98 of the ERA 1996:

> ... the determination of the question whether the dismissal is fair or unfair (having regard to the reason shown by the employer):
>
> (a) depends on whether, in the circumstances (including the size and administrative resources of the employer's undertaking), the employer acted reasonably or unreasonably in treating it as a sufficient reason for dismissing the employee; and
>
> (b) shall be determined in accordance with equity and the substantial merits of the case.

In *Iceland Frozen Foods v Jones* (1982), the EAT summed up the correct approach for the tribunal to adopt in answering the question posed by s 98(4) as follows:

- the starting point should always be the words of s 98(4);
- in applying the section, the tribunal must consider the reasonableness of the employer's conduct, not simply whether they (the members of the tribunal) consider the dismissal to be fair;
- in judging the reasonableness of the employer's conduct, a tribunal must not substitute its own decision as to what was the right course to adopt for that of the employer;
- in many (though not all) cases, there is a band of reasonable responses to the employee's conduct, within which one employer might reasonably take one view and another may quite reasonably take another;
- the function of the tribunal, as an industrial jury, is to determine whether, in the particular circumstances of each case, the decision to dismiss fell within the band of reasonable responses which a reasonable employer might have adopted. If the dismissal falls within the band, the dismissal is fair; if it falls outside the band, it is unfair.

Procedural fairness

The main requirements of the ACAS Code of Practice are:

- warnings (para 12);
- careful investigation by the employer (paras 10(I) and 11);
- an opportunity to state a case and a right to be accompanied (paras 10(F), 10(G) and 11);
- the right of appeal (paras 10(K) and 16).

Although the Code does not have statutory force, it emphasises the renewed importance that is being attached to procedural fairness.

By the late 1970s, there had been a dilution of procedural requirements. The high point in this trend was to be found in the test laid down by the EAT in *British Labour Pump Co Ltd v Byrne* (1979). This test allowed the employer to argue that an element of procedural unfairness (such as a failure to give a proper hearing) could be 'forgiven' if the employer could show that, on the balance of probabilities, even if a proper procedure had been complied with, the employee would still have been dismissed and the dismissal would still have been fair.

This test was overruled by the House of Lords in *Polkey v AE Dayton Services* (1987). In the speeches, there is a re-emphasis of the importance of following a fair procedure. In the view of Lord Bridge of Harwich:

> ... an employer having *prima facie* grounds to dismiss ... will, in the great majority of cases, not act reasonably in treating the reason as a sufficient reason for dismissal unless and until he has taken the steps, conveniently classified in most of the authorities as 'procedural', which are necessary in the circumstances of the case to justify that course of action.

Lord Mackay of Clashfern was of the opinion that what must be considered is what a reasonable employer would have had in mind at the time he decided to dismiss the employee(s):

> If the employer could reasonably have concluded, in the light of the circumstances known to him at the time of the dismissal, that consultation or warning would be useless, he might well act reasonably even if he did not observe the provisions of the code.

As a result of this decision, failure to follow a fair procedure may well lead to a finding of unfair dismissal in a much increased proportion of cases. However, it is clear that the 'no difference' test still has a significant part to play in reducing compensation awards (see *Rao v Civil Aviation Authority* (1994); *Red Bank Manufacturing Co Ltd v Meadows* (1992)).

The *Polkey* decision should also be viewed alongside the earlier House of Lords ruling in *West Midlands Co-operative Society Ltd v Tipton* (1986). As with *Polkey*, the point at issue was the precise scope of the *Devis v Atkins* principle. Ever since *Devis v Atkins* (1977), it was not clear whether and to what extent that decision prevented matters arising out of internal appeals from being considered by employment tribunals as part of their assessment of 'reasonableness'. In *Tipton*, the Lords confirmed that both the denial of a contractual right of appeal and matters arising out of an appeal, if one is held, can be taken into account by tribunals when they assess the reasonableness of the employer's conduct.

The Employment Act 2002, however, introduces a statutory dispute resolution procedure consisting of three stages:

Stage 1 The employer should in writing notify the employee of the issues in dispute, and invite the employee to a meeting.

Stage 2 The meeting between the employer and employee should take place before any action is decided upon. The employer should then advise the employee of any decision taken.

Stage 3 If the employee wishes to appeal against the decision taken, a further meeting should be arranged. However, the action decided upon may be undertaken prior to the appeal meeting taking place.

Failure by the employer to follow this statutory procedure may not render the dismissal unfair. It therefore appears that issues of procedure have less significance following the introduction of Employment Act 2002 (s 34), and *Polkey* may no longer be relied upon.

Stage 4: remedies

Remedies include:

- an order for reinstatement;
- an order for re-engagement;
- an award of compensation.

'Reinstatement' means putting the employee back into his own job as if the dismissal had never taken place. 'Re-engagement' is defined as putting the applicant into a similar job. Rights (such as the use of a company car) lost between dismissal and re-employment may be the subject of financial orders.

Compensation

The rules relating to the calculation of unfair dismissal compensation can be summarised as follows.

The basic award (s 119 of the ERA 1996)

An award of half, one or one and a half week's pay for each year of continuous service (depending on age), subject to a maximum of 20 years. A week's pay is calculated in accordance with ss 220–29 of the ERA 1996, and is based on gross pay. The term 'week's pay' is subject to a statutory maximum, which is normally amended on an annual basis.

Basic award and age

If aged	but less than	No of weeks' pay for each year
	22	$1/2$
22	41	1
41	65	$1^1/2$

Compensatory award

The tribunal may also make a compensatory award (s 123 of the ERA 1996). This is an amount which the tribunal considers 'just and equitable'. Both the basic and compensatory award may be reduced if the applicant contributed to his own dismissal or as a result of any conduct before dismissal. The maximum award under this head is £53,700, subject to review on an annual basis.

The aim of the award is to reimburse the employee for any financial loss experienced: interim loss of net earnings between the date of the dismissal and the tribunal hearing and future losses that he is likely to sustain, including wages, pensions and other fringe benefits. The amount must be 'just and equitable'. Sums are then deducted for, for example, contributory fault and failure to mitigate.

The additional award

This award is made where an order for reinstatement or re-engagement is not complied with. The award is between 26 and 52 weeks' pay.

6 Redundancy payments

See Pt XI of the Employment Rights Act (ERA) 1996 (ss 135–65). Payment is calculated in the same way as the basic award in unfair dismissal cases (see p 000), except that years worked while under the age of 18 do not count.

Pre-conditions for payment

To qualify for redundancy payments, the following are necessary:

- the person made redundant was an 'employee';
- he was continuously employed for a period of two years, ending with the 'relevant date';
- he was dismissed; and
- the dismissal was by reason of redundancy.

There is a presumption of redundancy (s 163(2)). Therefore, the burden of proof is on the employers to disprove redundancy.

Situations where no dismissal is deemed to have occurred

The following are situations in which no dismissal is deemed to have occurred:

- suitable offer of renewal or re-engagement;
- offers of suitable employment by associated companies;
- where there is a 'relevant transfer' of an undertaking.

Employees who leave prematurely

If an employee leaves employment, having been warned of the possibility of redundancy in the future, but before receiving notice of termination, there is no dismissal: *Morton Sundour Fabrics Ltd v Shaw* (1966).

Dismissal must be by reason of redundancy

'Redundancy' is defined in s 139 of the ERA 1996 as follows:

> For the purposes of this Act, an employee who is dismissed shall be taken to be dismissed by reason of redundancy if the dismissal is attributable wholly or mainly to:
>
> (a) the fact that his employer has ceased, or intends to cease:
>   (i) to carry on the business for the purposes of which the employee was employed by him; or
>   (ii) to carry on that business in the place where the employee was so employed; or
>
> (b) the fact that the requirements of that business:
>   (i) for employees to carry out work of a particular kind; or
>   (ii) for employees to carry out work of a particular kind in the place where the employee was so employed by the employer,
>
> have ceased or diminished or are expected to cease or diminish.

Dismissals for misconduct, including being on strike, are not dismissals for redundancy.

Definitional analysis of work of a particular kind

There is a redundancy situation where the amount of work remains the same but an event, such as a re-organisation, discloses that overstaffing exists. This is because the statutory definition requires a diminution in the number of employees to do work of a particular kind, as opposed to a diminution in the work itself: *McCrea v Cullen and Davidson* (1988).

In *Safeway Stores plc v Burrell* (1997), Mr Burrell, a petrol station manager, was told that there would be a re-organisation of the management structure and that the post of 'petrol station manager' would disappear. It was to be replaced by a new post of 'petrol filling station controller' at a lower salary. Existing postholders could apply for the management posts, although, as there were fewer posts than managers, there would be redundancies. Mr Burrell declined the invitation to apply and brought a complaint of unfair dismissal. He argued that the new job was essentially the same as the old one, so there was no redundancy situation. The employer contended that it was a genuine redundancy, or, alternatively, that there was justification for the dismissal on the basis of 'some other substantial reason'. The majority of the tribunal upheld Mr Burrell's claim. Many of the jobs he had actually done (the 'functional' test) were still required, albeit by someone with a different job title. The employment tribunal chair (in the minority) looked at what Mr Burrell's contract required (the 'contract' test) and concluded that the job he was employed to do no longer existed.

The EAT allowed the appeal and remitted the case for reconsideration by another tribunal. It held that the correct test involved three stages:

- Was the employee dismissed?
- If so, had the requirements of the business for employees to carry out work of a particular kind 'ceased or diminished' (or were they expected to do so)?
- If so, was the dismissal caused wholly or mainly by that state of affairs?

The key issue at stage (b), said the EAT, was whether there was a diminution in the business requirements for employees (note: 'employees' generally, not the employee specifically) and, in deciding that, tribunals should not introduce a 'contract' test whereby they just considered the specific tasks for which the applicant was employed. On this test see also *Shawkat v Nottingham City Hospital NHS Trust* (2001).

Bumping

'Bumping', or transferred redundancy, occurs when a person selected for redundancy is retained and another employee is dismissed in his place. In *Church v Lancashire NHS Trust* (1998), the EAT held that, as a matter of causation, the diminution or cessation in an employer's requirement for employees to carry out work of a particular kind must relate to the work carried out by the dismissed employee himself. Therefore, the EAT took the view that bumping does not fall within the statutory definition of redundancy.

However, the House of Lords, on appeal from the Northern Ireland case of *Murray v Foyle Meats Ltd* (1999), held that bumping was within the statutory definition of redundancy. Neither the 'contract' nor the 'functional' test was correct. One had to apply the pure words of the statute: has the employers' requirement that employees do work of a particular kind ceased or diminished? If so, was the dismissal attributable to that? The fundamental question, following *Murray,* is whether the dismissal was wholly or mainly attributable to a redundancy situation – if so, the dismissal is by way of redundancy.

Place where the employee was employed

The contractual approach has also been used to determine the 'place of employment'. This phrase has been interpreted to mean the place where the employee could be obliged to work under the terms of the contract of employment, not merely where the employee had been working prior to the instruction to move: *Sutcliffe v Hawker Siddeley Aviation* (1973); *UKAEA v Claydon* (1974). More recently, this conventional approach was challenged in *Bass Leisure Ltd v Thomas* (1994), where the EAT ruled that the place where an employee was employed for redundancy payment purposes does not necessarily extend to any place where he could be contractually required to work, but is to be established by a factual inquiry, taking into account the employee's fixed or changing places of work and any contractual terms which evidence or define the place of employment and its extent, but not terms which provide for the employee to be transferred. The decision of the Court of Appeal in *High Table Ltd v Horst* (1997) approved the 'factual or geographical' test, as formulated in *Bass Leisure*, rather than the contractual test. These decisions will often make it easier to establish redundancy and allow the employer the best of both worlds with a mobility clause. If there is a mobility clause within the contract and the employee refuses to move, there may well be a fair dismissal. If, however, the employer does not choose to rely on the mobility clause when the work ceases or diminishes at the existing locality, the employer can still rely on redundancy in spite of the clause.

An employment contract cannot be silent on the place of work. If there is no express term, there must be an implied term. The geographical scope of the implied term depends on the circumstances of the case. Relevant factors include the nature of the employer's business; whether the employee has been moved during the course of the employment; what the employee was told when the employment started; and whether there are any provisions to cover expenses when working away from home: *O'Brien v Associated Fire Alarms Ltd* (1968); *Stevenson v Teesside Bridge and Engineering Ltd* (1971); *Jones v Associated Tunnelling Co Ltd* (1981); *Courtaulds Northern Spinning Ltd v Sibson* (1988).

Re-organisation and redundancy

There is no redundancy if the job function remains the same, even though there has been a substantial alteration in terms and conditions:

- *North Riding Garages v Butterwick* (1967);
- *Vaux and Associated Brewers v Ward* (1969);
- *Chapman v Goonvean and Rostowrack China Clay* (1973);
- *Johnson v Nottinghamshire Combined Police Authority* (1974);
- *Lesney Products & Co Ltd v Nolan* (1977);
- cf *MacFisheries Ltd v Findlay* (1985).

The question to be asked, therefore, is whether the job itself has changed (= redundancy) or whether it is merely the way of doing the job which has changed (= question of adaptability).

Re-organisation and unfair dismissal

As the cases listed above illustrate, where re-organisation causes a change in the employee's terms and conditions of employment, these changes may not fall within the legal concept of redundancy because the work that the employee does is not diminished. Can the imposition of such changes amount to unfair dismissal? The test of fairness is not inevitably controlled by the contract of employment. As a result, the courts and tribunals have been prepared to hold as fair dismissal cases where the employee has refused to agree to a change in terms and conditions in line with the employer's perception of business efficacy: see *Hollister v National Union of Farmers* (1979); *St John of God v Brook* (1992).

Unreasonable refusal of suitable alternative employment

This will cause the employee to lose his right to a redundancy payment. The alternative must be objectively suitable. If so, whether the employee rejected it reasonably is assessed with regard to the particular employee. For example, the offer of a job in a 'floating pool' of teachers was not a suitable one for a head teacher because it reduced the status of the job: *Taylor v Kent CC* (1969). In respect of the second issue (that is, whether the refusal is reasonable or not), a move from Mayfair to an office above a sex shop in Soho was unreasonably refused by a female employee in *Fuller v Stephanie Bowman Ltd* (1977).

Trial periods

An employee who wishes to try out an alternative job is given a trial period of four weeks by statute (s 138). If, however, he has been dismissed for redundancy, there is both a common law period of a reasonable length and the four week statutory period.

Unfair redundancy dismissals

Dismissal for redundancy may be attacked as unfair on three grounds:

- ➲ trade union/non-trade union membership or activity (s 153 of TULR(C)A 1992);
- ➲ the reason for the redundancy selection was because of pregnancy or childbirth or because the employee had made health and safety complaints or asserted certain statutory rights (s 105 of the ERA 1996);

→ unreasonable redundancy under *Williams v Compair Maxam* (1982). Here, the EAT set out five principles of good industrial relations practice that should generally be followed when employees are represented by a recognised trade union:

(1) to give as much warning as possible;
(2) to consult with the union, particularly relating to the criteria to be applied in selection for redundancy;
(3) to adopt objective rather than subjective criteria for selection, for example, experience, length of service, attendance, etc;
(4) to select in accordance with the criteria, considering any representations made by the union regarding selection;
(5) to consider the possibility of re-deployment rather than dismissal.

Transfer of Undertakings (Protection of Employment) Regulations 1981 (SI 1981/1794)

These complex regulations, as amended from time to time, seek to fulfil the UK's obligations under EC law to give effect to EC Council Directive 77/187 (as amended by Directive 98/50), generally known as the Acquired Rights Directive. The regulations provide that, where an undertaking is transferred from person A to person B:

→ workers who are employed by A 'immediately before the transfer' automatically become the employees of B, retaining the same terms and conditions that they enjoyed with A;

→ B assumes A's rights and liabilities in relation to those employees;

- any collective and union recognition agreements are transferred;
- A must inform recognised trade unions of the consequences of the transfer;
- dismissal of an employee (whether before or after transfer) for any reason connected with the transfer is automatically unfair unless the reason is for an 'economic, technical or organisational reason entailing changes in the workforce', in which case the dismissal is fair if reasonable in the circumstances.

The parties cannot contract out of the regulations.

Relevant transfers

None of the provisions in the regulations operates unless there is a 'relevant transfer' under reg 3(1), that is:

> … a transfer from one person to another of an undertaking situated immediately before the transfer in the UK or a part of one which is so situated.

The Directive is wide enough to cover transfers of undertakings which are non-commercial in nature: see *Dr Sophie Redmond Stichting v Bartol* (1992).

It is probable that a mere transfer of assets which falls short of a transfer of an undertaking as a going concern will fall outside the regulations. The ECJ has enunciated the test as to whether a stable economic entity has been transferred. In *Schmidt v Spar und Leihkasse der Fruheren Amter Bordesholm, Kiel and Cronshagen* (1994), it held that there could be a transfer of contracted-out cleaning services, even where the services are performed by a single employee and there is no transfer of tangible assets. Contrast this approach to the ECJ's more recent finding in *Suzen v Zehnacker Gebaudereingung GmbH Krankenhaus-service* (1997) that an activity does not, in itself, constitute a stable economic entity. Consequently, the ECJ stated, the mere fact that a similar activity is carried on before and after the change of contractors does not mean that there is a transfer of undertaking.

In the case of a labour-intensive undertaking with no significant assets (for example, contract cleaning), the *Suzen* approach will mean that there will generally be no transfer unless the new contractor takes on the majority of the old contractor's staff (see also *Betts v Brintel Helicopters Ltd and KLM ERA Helicopters (UK) Ltd* (1997)). Such a ruling permits a firm which successfully tenders for a contract to avoid the application of the regulations by not taking on the transferor's employees. The Court of Appeal has sought to avoid this outcome by ruling that *Suzen* did not alter prior law as laid down in *Schmidt*: *ECM (Vehicle Delivery Service) Ltd v Cox* (1999); *Cheesman v R Brewer Contracts Ltd* (2001); *ADI (UK) Ltd v Willer* (2001).

Effect of a transfer on contracts of employment

On a relevant transfer, the employee takes with him the contractual rights, and claims against the transferor (such as sex discrimination) are transferred to the transferee. It is arguable that personal injury claims are also transferred.

It may be important to identify the precise time of the transfer because of the requirement that the employee must be employed by his old employer immediately before the transfer. This was a big issue in earlier cases, but is less problematic following the decision of the House of Lords in *Litster v Forth Dry Dock and Engineering Co Ltd* (1989). If the dismissal was connected to the transfer, then it will be caught by the regulations, irrespective of the precise timing of the dismissal (see also *P Bork International A/S v Forgeningen af Arbejdsledere i Danmark* (1989)).

Altering terms and conditions

In the joined cases of *Wilson and Others v St Helens BC; Meade and Baxendale v British Fuels Ltd* (1997), the crucial question was whether the Transfer of Undertakings (Protection of Employment) Regulations 1981 permit changes in the terms and conditions to be agreed between the transferee and employees whose work has been transferred. The EAT held that employees could not be bound by an agreement to vary their terms and conditions if the transfer of the undertaking was the reason for the change. In other words, employees could not be bound by a unilaterally imposed change, nor would they be bound by a consensual change. Ultimately, this was the position adopted by the House of Lords (see *Wilson v St Helens BC; Meade and Baxendale v British Fuels Ltd* (1998) (HL); see also *Credit Suisse First Boston (Europe) Ltd v Lister* (1998) (CA)).

Dismissal on a transfer of undertaking

Regulation 8(1) deems a dismissal caused by a transfer or for a reason connected with a transfer to be automatically unfair. This position is modified by reg 8(2), which allows the employer to argue that the dismissal was for an 'economic, technical or organisational reason entailing changes in the workforce of either the transferor or the transferee before or after the relevant transfer'. Such dismissals are fair provided they pass the statutory test of reasonableness. It is now clear that, if the employer does successfully establish the economic, technical or organisational (ETO) defence, an employee can claim a redundancy payment if redundancy was the reason for the transfer: *Gorictree Ltd v Jenkinson* (1984).

The scope of the ETO defence was considered by the Court of Appeal in *Berriman v Delabole Slate Ltd* (1985).

Here, it was held that, in order to come within reg 8(2), the employer must show that the change in the workforce is part of the economic, technical or organisational reason for dismissal. It must be an objective of the employer's plan to achieve changes in the workforce, not just a possible consequence of the plan. So, where an employee resigned, following a transfer, because the transferee employer proposed to remove his guaranteed weekly wage so as to bring his pay into line with the transferee's existing workforce, the reason behind the plan was to produce uniform terms and conditions and was not in any way intended to reduce the number of the workforce.

Exclusions

The regulations do not cover rights and liabilities relating to the provision of occupational pension schemes, which relate to benefits for old age, invalidity or survivors (reg 7 and see *Walden Engineering Co Ltd v Warrener* (1993)). Criminal liabilities are not transferred.

The regulations apply only to the transfer of an undertaking from one legal person to another. Examples include the transfer of leases and franchises and the outsourcing of services (subject to *Suzen* (1997)). They do not apply to the transfer of shares in a company which carries on the undertaking: see *Brookes and Others v Borough Care Services and CLS Care Services Ltd* (1998).

In *Katsikas v Konstantidis* (1993), the ECJ held that an employee could not be transferred to the employment of a new employer without his consent. As a result, s 33(4) of the Trade Union Reform and Employment Rights Act 1993 has amended reg 5 so as to provide that the transfer of the contract of employment will not occur if the employee informs the transferor/transferee that he objects to becoming employed by the transferee. In that event, the transfer will terminate the employee's contract of employment with the transferor, but he will not be treated for any purpose as having been dismissed by the transferor. This exception might be of importance in the context of restrictive/garden leave covenants, where continuing obligations will dissolve.

7 Collective labour relations

The main features of post-war collective labour law

- ➔ Traditional approach dating from 1906: State non-intervention in industrial relations: legal abstentionism, voluntarism, collective *laissez-faire*. Exceptions included health and safety laws. Modern statutory intervention began in mid-1960s and gathered pace in 1970s. EC law began to take effect in late 1970s.
- ➔ Very few statutory props to support collective bargaining, the means by which management and unions reached agreements: no statutory right to union recognition (with the exception of the 'social contract' era 1974–79); collective bargains not legally enforceable.
- ➔ Trade union immunities as opposed to positive rights.
- ➔ 1979–97: new policies of intervention and restriction: narrowing of strike immunities; statutory right for union members against unjustifiable discipline by their union; legal outlawing of the closed shop; abolition of wages councils and the Fair Wages Resolution.
- ➔ 1997: Labour Government's White Paper, *Fairness at Work* (May 1998), proposed a widening of individual rights, but did not significantly alter the framework of restriction of trade union rights put in place by the previous Conservative administrations (with the major exception of introducing a statutory right of recognition where the majority of the relevant workforce wishes it: the right formed part of the Employment Relations Act 1999). Statutory minimum wage was introduced.
- ➔ Both trade unions and statutory intervention can be seen as methods by which employers and the State sought to

equalise the bargaining power of employers and employees. However, for a long time, unions did not want the State to intervene, and it is only in the last 20 years that this attitude has changed.

Industrial action

In the UK, there is no positive right to strike. Instead, there is merely a system of immunities from liability which offer a limited shield of protection to trade unions and strike organisers. This shield, always vulnerable to attack by an unsympathetic judiciary, has been weakened still further by the changes introduced by the Governments since 1980. Moreover, those workers who take strike or other industrial action may have some or all of their pay 'docked' and incur the risk of dismissal, with a limited right to challenge its fairness before an employment tribunal.

The changes to collective labour law introduced during the 1980s have been put together in one Act of Parliament: TULR(C)A 1992. The relevant provisions of that Act are referred to below.

Sanctions against individual strikers

Dismissal: limited right to claim unfair dismissal for those taking industrial action

See ss 237 and 238 of TULR(C)A 1992, as amended by the Employment Relations Act 1999.

Leading cases

The leading decisions with regard to unfair dismissal claims where industrial action has been taken are:

- *Faust v Power Packing Casemakers Ltd* (1983);
- *P&O European Ferries (Dover) Ltd v Byrne* (1989);
- *Coates v Modern Methods and Materials Ltd* (1982).

Dismissal of unofficial strikers is automatically fair, or, better put, the tribunal has no jurisdiction to hear the case. The same is true of official strikers unless the employers selectively re-engage or selectively dismiss some of the strikers within three months of the start of the action or dismiss any strikers within eight weeks (or after that period if the employers have taken no steps to resolve the dispute).

Possible loss of redundancy payments

See s 140(1) and (2) of the ERA 1996, which deal with misconduct. A strike is misconduct.

Suing for breach of contract

See *National Coal Board v Galley* (1958).

Deductions from wages of those taking industrial action

The House of Lords' decision in *Miles v Wakefield MDC* (1987) upholds the principle of 'no work, no pay' as the basis for the mutual obligations between employer and employee.

See *Wiluszynski v Tower Hamlets LBC* (1989) (an employer who refuses to accept partial performance of an employee's contractual obligations can withhold all wages payable during the period of the industrial action); see also *British Telecommunications plc v Ticehurst* (1992).

Legal action against the trade union and strike organisers

A three stage framework of analysis.

Stage 1

Does the industrial action give rise to civil liability at common law?

Stage 2

If so, is there an immunity from liability provided by s 219 of TULR(C)A 1992?

Stage 3

If so, has that immunity now been removed by virtue of the changes introduced by the Employment Acts of 1980, 1982, 1988 and 1990; the Trade Union Act 1984; TURERA 1993, and now contained within TULR(C)A?

Stage 1: civil liabilities for industrial action

Industrial action and how it affects the contract of employment

The contract of employment is not suspended during a strike. The traditionally accepted view is that a strike is a breach of contract, that is, a breach of the obligation on the part of the employee to be ready and willing to work. This is so even if strike notice has been given: this is merely notice of impending breach.

Most other forms of industrial action short of a strike also amount to contractual breaches. If workers 'boycott' (refuse to carry out) certain work, they are in breach for refusing to comply with a reasonable order. A 'go slow' or 'work to rule' probably breaks an implied term not to frustrate the commercial objectives of the business (see *Secretary of State for Employment v ASLEF (No 2)* (1972)).

An overtime ban will also certainly amount to breach of contract if the employer is entitled under the contract to demand overtime, but not necessarily if overtime is voluntary on the part of the employee (see *Faust v Power Packing Casemakers Ltd* (1983)).

As we have seen, where the industrial action does constitute breach, the employer may summarily dismiss or sue for damages. But, in relation to strike organisers, the true significance of a finding of breach is that it constitutes the 'unlawful means' element necessary in certain economic torts (see below).

The economic torts

It is possible to place the torts relevant to industrial action under four broad headings:

- inducement of breach of contract;
- interference with contract, trade or business;
- intimidation;
- conspiracy.

Inducement of breach of contract

This is the main economic tort and derives from *Lumley v Gye* (1853). The inducement may take one of two forms: direct or indirect. There is a possible defence of justification.

Direct inducement

Occurs where the defendant induces a third party to break an existing contract which the third party has with the claimant, who thereby suffers loss. It may help to conceptualise this and other torts if the position is expressed in diagrammatic form.

Inducement	*Breach of employment contract*	
Ann ⟶	**Brenda** ⟶	**Capital plc**
(Union official)	(Employee)	(Employer)

In the above example, Brenda is employed by Capital plc. Ann, a trade union officer, instructs her to strike. Ann is directly inducing Brenda to break her contract with Capital and is, therefore, committing a tort.

The necessary elements of this form of the tort are:

- knowledge of the contract;
- intention to cause its breach;
- evidence of an inducement;
- actual breach.

Unlawful means are not needed.

Note also that this form of the tort can be committed where a union puts pressure directly on one of the employer's suppliers to cease delivery of vital supplies, thereby inducing breach of a commercial contract. However, boycotting the employer in dispute usually arises as the second form of the tort, that is, indirect inducement.

Indirect inducement

Occurs where the unlawful means are used to render performance of the contract by one of the parties impossible.

Breach of employment contract		*Breach of commercial contract*	
Ann ⟹	**Brenda** ⟹	**Capital plc** ⟹	**Delta plc**

In this example, Delta plc's workers are in dispute with their employer. Capital plc is a supplier of Delta. Brenda is employed by Capital as a lorry driver. Ann, a union official, persuades Brenda not to make deliveries to Delta. Not only has Ann directly induced Brenda to break her contract of employment with Capital, she has also used unlawful means and indirectly induced a breach of commercial contract between Capital and Delta (*DC Thomson v Deakin* (1952)).

Interference with contract, trade or business

It will be unlawful to interfere with a contract short of breach, for example, by preventing performance in cases where the contract contains a *force majeure* clause exempting a party in breach from liability to pay damages: see the county court judgment in *Falconer v ASLEF and NUR* (1986). There must be unlawful means, such as breach of statutory duty.

More recently, it would appear that this head of liability is even broader in scope, encompassing any intentional use of unlawful means aimed at interfering with the claimant's trade or business, regardless of the existence or not of a contract: *Merkur Island Shipping Corp v Laughton* (1983).

Intimidation

The tort of intimidation may take the form of compelling a person, by threats of unlawful action, to do some act which causes him loss; or intimidating other persons, by threats of unlawful action, with the intention and effect of causing loss to a third party. Prior to 1964, it was assumed that the tort was confined to threats of physical violence but, in that year, the House of Lords held that threats to break a contract were encompassed by the tort: *Rookes v Barnard* (1964).

Conspiracy

This tort may take two forms:

- ◑ conspiracy to commit an unlawful act: a conspiracy to commit a crime or tort is clearly included in this category;
- ◑ conspiracy to injure by lawful means.

It is the second form of conspiracy which is the greatest threat to strikers, because it makes it unlawful for two or more people to do something which would have been quite lawful if performed by an individual. A conspiracy to injure is simply an agreement to cause deliberate loss to another without justification. The motives or purposes of the defendants are important. If the predominant purpose is to injure the claimant, the conspiracy is actionable. If, on the other hand, the principal aim is to achieve a legitimate goal, the action is not unlawful, even if, in so doing, the claimant suffers injury. Whilst it took the courts some time to accept trade union objectives as legitimate (see *Quinn v Leathem* (1901)), later decisions adopted a more liberal stance (see *Crofter Hand Woven Harris Tweed Co v Veitch* (1942)). As a result, this form of the tort does not pose the threat it once did to trade union activities.

Stage 2: the immunities

These are now contained in s 219 of TULR(C)A 1992.

Inducement to breach of contract

Under the Trade Disputes Act 1906, the immunity for inducements to breach in contemplation or furtherance of a trade dispute only extended to contracts of employment. This had allowed the courts in the 1960s to find ways of holding trade unionists liable for inducing breaches of commercial contracts: see *Stratford v Lindley* (1965).

In the mid-1970s, immunity was extended to cover the breach of 'any' contract. The relevant provision states that an act done by a person in contemplation or furtherance of a trade dispute shall not be actionable in tort on the ground only 'that it induces another person to break a contract or interferes or induces any other person to interfere with its performance': see, now, s 219(1)(a) of TULR(C)A 1992.

As we shall see, however, it is important to view this immunity in the context of subsequent legislative developments. Section 219(1)(a) provides a *prima facie* immunity, but this immunity may be lost in certain instances, namely, by taking unlawful secondary action; engaging in secondary picketing; enforcing trade union membership; or taking 'official' industrial action without first having called a secret ballot.

Interference with contract, trade or business

Section 219(1)(a) provides an immunity against the tort of interference with contract. It does not, however, offer any explicit protection against the wider 'genus' tort of interference with trade or business by unlawful means. As a result, it is of crucial importance to discover whether an act which is immune by virtue of s 219 (inducement to breach of contract, for example) may nonetheless constitute the 'unlawful means' for the tort of interference with trade or business. Before the passage of the Employment Act 1980, s 13(3) of TULRA 1974 (as amended) stated that, 'for the avoidance of doubt', acts already given immunity could not found the unlawful means element of other torts. When the 1980 statute repealed s 13(3), the legal position became confused. However, it would appear that the correct view is that the repeal of s 13(3) has not changed the position. According to the House of Lords in *Hadmor Productions Ltd v Hamilton* (1982), s 13(3) merely confirmed what was obvious from s 13(1), that is, inducement is 'not actionable'. So, if the unlawful means are immune, no liability can arise in tort.

Intimidation

This immunity is contained in s 219(1)(b) of TULR(C)A 1992, which states that an act done by a person in contemplation or furtherance of a trade dispute shall not be actionable in tort on the ground only:

... that it consists of his threatening that a contract (whether one to which he is a party or not) will be broken, or its performance interfered with, or that he will induce another person to break a contract or to interfere with its performance.

Conspiracy

Section 219(2) now provides the immunity against simple conspiracy, which was originally contained in the Trade Disputes Act 1906.

The trade dispute immunity

In order to gain the protection of the immunities, the individual must be acting *in contemplation or furtherance of a trade dispute.* This is known as the 'golden formula'. For analytical purposes, four questions should be asked in order to determine whether the industrial action qualifies:

- Is it between the correct parties? See below.
- Is there a dispute? Note that there may still be a dispute even if the employer is willing to concede to the demands of the union (s 244(4)). Thus, if an employer ceases to supply another company on receiving a threat of strike action by its workforce if it continues to supply, there is still a dispute
- Is the subject matter of the dispute wholly or mainly related to one or more of the matters listed in s 244(1)? See below.
- Is the action in contemplation or furtherance of a trade dispute?

A trade dispute must relate wholly or mainly to a matter in s 244(1). These matters include the terms of employment, discipline, membership and non-membership of a union and dismissal.

⟳ A trade dispute must be 'between workers and *their* employers' (emphasis added), not between 'employers and workers', which was the previous position. The Act does not allow trade unions and employers' associations to be regarded as parties to a trade dispute in their own right (cf *NWL v Woods* (1979) and see s 244(1) and (5) of TULR(C)A 1992)).

⟳ Disputes between 'workers and workers' are now omitted from the 'trade dispute' definition. Whilst this means that disputes not involving an employer are unlawful, in practice, it is rare for an employer not to be party to inter-union disputes. A demarcation dispute between unions will usually involve a dispute with an employer regarding terms and conditions of employment.

⟳ A trade dispute must relate 'wholly or mainly' to terms and conditions of employment and the other matters listed as legitimate in s 244 of TULR(C)A 1992.

⟳ Since 1982, disputes relating to matters occurring outside the UK are excluded from the immunity, unless the UK workers taking action in furtherance of the dispute are likely to be affected by its outcome in terms of the matters listed in s 244 (see s 244(3)).

Political disputes are not 'trade' disputes. An example is a strike against the Government's economic policy (see *Mercury Communications Ltd v Scott-Garner* (1983)).

In contemplation or furtherance

In *Express Newspapers Ltd v McShane* (1980), the main thrust of the decision was that, if a person taking the action honestly believed that it would further the trade dispute, then this is all that matters: there is no room for an objective test: see also *Duport Steels Ltd v Sirs* (1980). Acts are not done within the golden formula once the dispute is at an end.

Stage 3: removal of the immunities

The scope of the immunities has been restricted by the legislation of the 1980s: the Employment Acts of 1980, 1982, 1988 and 1990; and the Trade Union Act 1984. In this section, we examine the restriction of secondary action; the provisions removing immunity in respect of actions aimed at enforcing the closed shop or trade union recognition on an employer; the loss of immunity for unlawful picketing; the requirements for secret ballots before industrial action; and industrial action taken in support of dismissed 'unofficial strikers'.

Statutory control of secondary action

Secondary action is not considered lawful action, and will not be protected by the 'golden formula'. The main exception to this is the situation detailed in the indirect form of the tort of inducement to breach of contract.

Section 224(4) seeks to limit any attempt to extend the notion of the primary employer. It states that an employer is not to be regarded as party to a dispute between another employer and its workers. This would appear to confirm the thinking of the House of Lords in *Dimbleby & Sons Ltd v National Union of Journalists* (1984) that an employer, even though associated with the employer involved in the primary dispute, was not to be regarded as a party to that dispute.

The other issue of secondary action concerns picketing: the basic immunity of s 219 only applies if the picket is acting lawfully within s 220, of which the main requirement is that workers may only picket their own place of work. Even if the workers do picket their own place of work, their actions may still amount to secondary action because they may induce a breach of the contracts of employment of the employees of other employers.

Unlawful picketing

Unlawful picketing, such as picketing a place other than one's own place of work, will not attract immunity under s 219: see s 219(3) of TULR(C)A 1992.

Enforcing union membership

The Employment Act 1988 further curbed the closed shop. Section 10 removed the immunities contained in s 13 of TULRA 1974 (as amended) from primary industrial action where the reason, or one of the reasons, for the action is that the employer is employing, has employed or might employ a person who is not a member of a trade union or that the employer is failing, has failed or might fail to discriminate against such a person. Section 11 made it unfair for an employer to dismiss an employee or to subject him to a detriment on the ground of the employee's non-membership of a union or particular union. In both of the situations covered by ss 10 and 11, the fact that the closed shop has been approved in a ballot is irrelevant: s 222 of TULR(C)A 1992.

Section 14 of the Employment Act 1982 withdrew the immunity where the reason for the industrial action is to compel another employer to 'recognise, negotiate or consult' one or more trade unions or to force the employer to discriminate in contract or tendering on the ground of union membership or non-membership in the contracting or tendering concern: see, now, s 225 of TULR(C)A 1992.

Secret ballots before industrial action

See ss 226–35 of TULR(C)A 1992.

Official industrial action will only attract the immunity offered by s 219 of TULR(C)A 1992 if the majority of union members likely to be called upon to take industrial action has supported that action in a properly conducted ballot. There are stringent rules as to when a ballot is so conducted. For example, there must be an independent scrutineer. The requirements for a lawful ballot and the ways in which a union can be held to be vicariously responsible for industrial action underwent considerable additions and modifications as a result of the Employment Acts of 1988 and 1990. To supplement these requirements, in 1991, the Department of Employment issued a Code of Practice on *Trade Union Ballots on Industrial Action*. On 17 November 1995 the new Code of Practice on *Industrial Action Ballots Notice to Employers* replaced the 1991 version. The very latest version was published in September 2000 to take account of changes introduced by the Employment Relations Act 1999. Breach of the Code does not, of itself, give rise to civil or criminal liability, but courts and tribunals must, where relevant, take it into account as evidence of good industrial relations practice. Some guidance through the complexities of the law in this area will now be offered.

When is a ballot required?

A ballot is only required in respect of an 'act done by a trade union'. An act is taken to have been authorised (beforehand) or endorsed (afterwards) by a trade union if it was done, authorised or endorsed by:

- any person who is empowered by the rules so to do;
- the principal executive committee or the president; or
- any other committee of the union or any official of the union (whether employed by it or not).

See s 20(2) of TULR(C)A 1992.

A union may repudiate the purported authorisation or endorsement by the third group, viz, other committees and officials, but can never repudiate the actions of the principal executive committee, president, general secretary or those acting under the rules. The requirements for an effective repudiation are far more stringent and complicated as a result of changes introduced by the Employment Act 1990. To escape liability, the action must be repudiated by the principal executive committee, president or general secretary as soon as reasonably practicable. Furthermore:

- written notice of the repudiation must be given to the committee or official in question without delay; and
- the union 'must do its best' to give individual written notice of the fact and date of repudiation, without delay:
    - to every member of the union who the union has reason to believe is taking part, or might otherwise take part, in industrial action as a result of the act; and
    - to the employer of every such member (see, now, s 21(2) of TULR(C)A 1992).

Should these requirements not be complied with, the repudiation will be treated as ineffective. In addition, there is no repudiation if the principal executive committee, president or general secretary subsequently 'behaves in a manner which is inconsistent with the purported repudiation'.

At this stage, it is important to emphasise the fundamental point that, whilst a properly conducted ballot is vital to maintain the protection of the immunities for any action authorised or endorsed by the union, a lawful ballot will not *per se* accord immunity to the action if it is unlawful for other reasons, for example, secondary action or action to enforce the closed shop.

Ballot requirements

Official industrial action will only attract immunity if the following conditions are met.

Separate ballots for each workplace

The requirement for separate ballots (ss 228(1) and 228A of TULR(C)A 1992) is subject to the following major exceptions:

- where the union reasonably believed that all the members had the same workplace;
- where there is some factor:
  - which relates to the terms, conditions or occupational description of each member entitled to vote;
  - which that member has in common with some or all members of the union entitled to vote.

This allows a trade union to hold a single aggregated ballot covering members from different places of work if all belong to a complete bargaining unit, for example, all electricians or all members employed by a particular employer. If you can make sense of this highly convoluted provision, you will also note that there does not have to be a factor which is common to all voters. There can be several factors, each of which is common to some, for example, all skilled and semi-skilled grades, all part time workers and electricians. The union must ballot all its members who possess the same relevant factor. So, for example, if it wishes to conduct a ballot of part time employees employed by a particular employer, it cannot ballot only those part time employees at workplace A, excluding part time employees at workplace B.

Ballot papers

The ballot paper must ask either whether the voter is prepared to take part or continue to take part in a strike, or whether the voter is prepared to take part or continue to take part in action short of a strike, or it may ask both questions separately. The voter must be required to answer 'yes' or 'no' to each question and the questions must not be rolled into one: see *Post Office v Union of Communication Workers* (1990). A strike is defined as a 'concerted stoppage of work' (s 246 of TULR(C)A 1992).

The ballot paper must also specify the identity of the person or persons authorised to call upon members to take industrial action in the event of a vote in favour. This person need not be authorised under the rules of the union, but he must be someone who comes within s 20(2) and (4) of TULR(C)A 1992. Section 20(2) provides that ballot papers must also name an independent scrutineer.

Conduct of the ballot

The ballot must comply with ss 227, 230, 232A and 232B of TULR(C)A 1992, as to equal entitlement to vote, secrecy, non-interference by the union's officials, etc. As a result of s 17 of TURERA 1993, the union now has no choice and must conduct a postal ballot (see, now, s 230(2) of TULR(C)A)). Section 227(1) provides that all those whom the union might reasonably believe will be induced to take part, or to continue to take part, in the strike or industrial action should be entitled to vote. Section 232A provides that that requirement is not satisfied where a trade union member who is called out on strike 'was denied entitlement to vote in a ballot' (see *RJB Mining (UK) Ltd v National Union of Mineworkers* (1997)). Section 230(3) relates to the opportunity to vote and provides that, 'so far as is reasonably practicable, every person who is entitled to vote in the ballot must [be given an opportunity to do so]' (*British Railways Board v NUR* (1989)). Voting must be carried out by marking a paper (s 229(1)).

Timing of the industrial action

The normal rule is that the action must be called within four weeks, beginning with the date of the ballot (s 234(1)). By the Employment Relations Act 1999, that period may be extended to eight weeks if the the union and management agree. Under s 234(2) of TULR(C)A 1992, a union may now apply for an extension of time to allow for the period during which they were prohibited by a court injunction from calling the action. An application has to be made 'forthwith upon the prohibition ceasing to have effect' and no application may be made after the end of the period of eight weeks, beginning with the date of the ballot.

The ballot paper must identify the person or persons authorised to call for industrial action (see above) and, indeed, industrial action will only be regarded as having the support of the ballot if called by this 'specified person' (s 233(1)). Finally, there must be no authorisation or endorsement of the action before the date of the ballot.

TURERA 1993 (as amended by the Employment Relations Act 1999) introduced the following additional requirements:

- once a ballot has produced a majority in favour of (continuing with) industrial action, a union is required to give the employer seven days' written notice of any industrial action to which the ballot relates. The notice has to contain information which enables the employers to make plans, and identify on what specific date the industrial action will begin;
- where a union proposes to call for intermittent action, such as a series of one-day strikes, it is required to give at least seven days' notice of each day or other separate period of industrial action;
- moreover, if the union suspends or withdraws its support for the action, further notice is required before any subsequent call to resume the action (see, now, s 234A of TULR(C)A 1992).

TURERA 1993 also gave employers the right to receive the following information:

- notice of intent to hold the ballot, with details of which workers will be entitled to vote, and of the voting procedure to be adopted in respect of those workers;
- a sample copy of the ballot paper, to enable the employer to know which questions will be asked and what other information will appear on the ballot paper; and
- the same details of the result as the law requires to be given to the union's members, and a copy of the report of the independent scrutineer for the ballot.

See, now, ss 226A, 231A and 231B of TULR(C)A 1992.

Member's statutory right to prevent unballoted action

Whilst the failure to hold a ballot will result in the loss of immunities, the Employment Act 1988 created an additional legal consequence. Where a trade union authorises or endorses 'industrial action' without first holding a ballot, one of its members who has been, or is likely to be, induced to take action may apply to the High Court for an order requiring the union to withdraw the authorisation or reverse the effect of its authorisation or endorsement: see, now, s 62 of TULR(C)A 1992.

Industrial action in support of dismissed 'unofficial strikers'

The Employment Act 1990 removed the limited unfair dismissal protection to 'unofficial' strikers (see, now, s 237 of TULR(C)A 1992). In order to strengthen the employer's position in such a situation, the 1990 Act removed the statutory immunity from any industrial action if 'the reason, or one of the reasons, for doing it is the fact or belief' that an employer has selectively dismissed one or more of the employees who were taking unofficial action (see, now, s 223 of TULR(C)A 1992).

Civil remedies and enforcement

The citizen's right of action

Any individual may apply to the High Court if a union or another person has performed an unlawful act to induce a person to take part in unlawful industrial action and that action does, or is likely to, prevent or reduce the quality of goods or services supplied to him (s 235A of TULR(C)A 1992). The court order instructs the defendant to desist.

Injunctions

An injunction is an order requiring the defendant to cease a particular course of action (a negative injunction) or, in its mandatory form, requiring the defendant to *do* something. The most frequent form of order in industrial disputes is the interlocutory injunction, requiring the organisers to call off the industrial action pending full trial of the action. The award of such an injunction may break the strike.

It used to be the case that, in order to be granted interim relief, the claimant had to establish a *prima facie* case. However, in *American Cyanamid Co v Ethicon Ltd* (1975) (a case involving patents law), the House of Lords substituted a less arduous test: namely, whether there is 'a serious issue' to be tried.

Additionally, the claimant must show that the defendant's conduct is causing him irreparable harm: harm that cannot be remedied by a subsequent award of damages (the 'status quo' concept).

Finally, the claimant must convince the court that the harm being suffered by him is greater than will be incurred by the defendants if they are ordered to cease their activities pending full trial (the 'balance of convenience' test).

The application of these tests generally produced a favourable result for the claimant employer. In determining the status quo and balance of convenience tests, it is easy to quantify the economic loss to an employer as a result of a strike, but it is far more difficult to assess the enormous damage that can be done to the union's bargaining position if the injunction is granted. This, together with the fact that interlocutory relief can be obtained on affidavit evidence at very short notice and without the defendants even having an opportunity to answer the complaint, meant that the process was very much tilted in favour of management.

Section 221 of TULR(C)A 1992 contains two provisions which seek to redress the imbalance:

- ⤷ s 221(1) requires reasonable steps to be taken to give notice of the application and an opportunity to be heard for a party likely to put forward a trade dispute defence;
- ⤷ s 221(2) provides that, where a party against whom an interlocutory injunction is sought claims that he acted in contemplation or furtherance of a trade dispute, the court shall have regard to the likelihood of that party succeeding in establishing a trade dispute defence. This was an attempt to mitigate the effects of *Cyanamid* in labour injunction cases.

See Lord Diplock's change of attitude between *NWL v Woods* (1979) and *Dimbleby & Sons Ltd v National Union of Journalists* (1984).

Breach of an injunction is a contempt of court. A fine for contempt is unlimited; it is not subject to the caps detailed in the next section.

Damages

Probably the most significant change in the structure of labour law during the 1980s was the Employment Act 1982. This made it possible to sue a trade union for unlawful industrial action. In doing this, the Act 'broke the mould' of British labour law, which had been used, but for the brief interlude of the Industrial Relations Act 1971, since 1906.

A union will be held vicariously liable for the unlawful industrial action of its membership where such action was authorised or endorsed by those identified in s 20(2) of TULR(C)A 1992.

Limits on damages awarded against trade unions in actions in tort

Section 22 of TULR(C)A 1992 places limits on the amounts which can be awarded against trade unions in actions brought against them where they have authorised or endorsed unlawful industrial action. The limits, which depend on the size of the trade union, are as follows:

- £10,000 for unions with fewer than 5,000 members;
- £50,000 for unions between 5,000 and fewer than 25,000 members;
- £125,000 for unions with more than 25,000 but fewer than 100,000 members;
- £250,000 if the union has 100,000 or more members.

These limits apply in 'any proceedings in tort brought against a trade union'. The effect of this phrase is that, where a union is sued by various claimants (for example, the employer in dispute, customers, suppliers, etc) for the damages caused to them by the unlawful action, then the maximum will be applied to them separately.

Picketing

Civil actions and criminal prosecutions may arise as a result of picketing.

The freedom to picket

As with strike action, English law provides no right to picket. Instead, it offers an extremely limited immunity from civil and criminal liability. This is now contained in s 220 of TULR(C)A 1992. Section 220(1)(a) states that:

> It shall be lawful for a person in contemplation or furtherance of a trade dispute to attend:
> (a) at or near his own place of work; or
> (b) if he is an official of a trade union, at or near the place of work of a member of that union whom he is accompanying and whom he represents, for the purposes only of communicating information or peacefully persuading any person to work or abstain from working.

Picketing will only receive the protection of the immunities if the pickets are attending at or near their own workplace. There is no right to stop vehicles. So called 'secondary picketing' was rendered unlawful by the Employment Act 1980. Flying pickets are also unlawful. There is no statutory definition of 'place of work'. However, the Code of Practice on *Picketing*, published in 1980 to accompany the amendments to the Employment Act 1980, and revised in 1992, offers the following guidance:

> The law does not enable a picket to attend lawfully at an entrance to, or exit from, any place of work other than his own. This applies even, for example, if those working at the other place of work are employed by the same employer or are covered by the same collective bargaining arrangements as the picket [para 18].

See *Rayware Ltd v TGWU* (1989).

The Act provides three exceptions to the 'own place of work' requirement:

- if workers normally work at more than one place (mobile workers) or if it is impractical to picket their place of work (for example, an oil rig), the section allows them to picket the place where their work is administered by the employer (s 220(2));
- workers who are dismissed during the dispute in question are permitted to picket their former place of work (s 220(3));
- as will be seen from s 220(1)(b), a trade union official may attend at any place of work, provided that:
  - he is accompanying a member or members of his trade union who are picketing at their own place of work; and
  - he personally represents those members within the trade union. An official – whether lay or full time – is regarded, for this purpose, as representing only those members he has been specifically appointed or elected to represent. So, it is lawful for a regional official to attend a picket at any place within that region, whereas a shop steward can only picket the workplace of the work group that he represents (see s 220(4)).

Civil liabilities

The economic torts

Without the protection of the immunities, picketing will generally result in an economic tort being committed. If workers assemble at the entrance to a workplace and attempt to persuade other employees not to work, the pickets could be liable for inducing a breach of contracts of employment. However, provided the picketing is lawful within s 220, the general immunity provided by s 219, in respect of tortious liability, applies: see s 219(3).

Private nuisance

Private nuisance is an unlawful interference with an individual's use or enjoyment or use of his land. Unreasonable interference with that right by, for example, blocking an access route to the employer's property, may give rise to a cause of action. So, even though the pickets stand outside the employer's premises, they may be liable for the tort of private nuisance.

Picketing which exceeds the bounds of peacefully obtaining or communicating information may involve liability for private nuisance. However, there is still doubt as to whether peaceful picketing itself amounts to a nuisance when not protected by the 'golden formula': see *Lyons v Wilkins* (1896); *Mersey Dock and Harbour Co Ltd v Verrinder* (1982); cf *Ward Lock & Co v Operative Printers' Assistants' Society* (1906); *Hubbard v Pitt* (1975) (*per* Lord Denning MR).

Thomas v NUM (South Wales Area) (1985)

Two important points arise from this decision:

⮕ private nuisance is concerned with interference with the use of or enjoyment of land in which the claimant has an interest. In this case, a species of the tort was held to extend to interference with the right to use the highway;

⮕ the terms of the injunction granted by the court restricted picketing at the collieries to peacefully communicating and obtaining information in numbers not exceeding six. This number is not a purely arbitrary figure – it comes from the Code of Practice on *Picketing* which advises that (para 51):

… pickets and their organisers should ensure that, in general, the number of pickets does not exceed six at any entrance to a workplace; frequently, a smaller number will be appropriate.

This would suggest that the judge was using the guidance in the Code to fix the parameters of lawful picketing. If this view is correct, then any picketing numbering more than six will lose the immunity offered by s 220 and will be tortious.

Trespass

Section 220 of the Trade Union and Labour Relations (Consolidation) Act 1992

Picketing is lawful where pickets attend 'at or near' their own place of work. To mount a picket *on* the employer's land without consent will mean that the immunity will be forfeited and that the tort of trespass has been committed: see *British Airports Authority v Ashton* (1983). Special damage is necessary and only the highway owners may sue.

Criminal liabilities

Whilst it is important to grasp the range of possible civil liabilities which may attach to certain types of picketing, it is the criminal law which is of the greatest practical significance in terms of control of the activity.

Obstructing a police officer in the execution of his duty

If a police officer reasonably apprehends that a breach of the peace is likely to occur, he has the right and duty at common law to take reasonable steps to prevent it. If the officer is obstructed in the exercise of this duty, an offence is committed: s 96(3) of the Police Act 1996. In practice, this gives the police a wide discretion to control picketing. While there must be an objective apprehension that a breach of the peace is a real – as opposed to a remote – possibility, the courts tend to accept the officer's assessment of the situation: see *Piddington v Bates* (1960); *Moss v McLachlan* (1985).

Obstruction of the highway

Section 137 of the Highways Act 1980

Under this provision, it is an offence to wilfully obstruct free passage along a highway without lawful authority or excuse. Before the offence is established, there must be proof of an unreasonable user of the highway. This is a question of fact and depends upon all the circumstances, including the length of time the obstruction continues, the place where it occurs, its purpose and whether it causes an actual as opposed to a potential obstruction (*Nagy v Weston* (1965)). It would appear that peaceful picketing carried out in the manner envisaged by s 15 of TULR(C)A 1992 and within the numbers advised by the Code will be held to be a reasonable user. If, however, these boundaries are crossed, the offence will be committed; as where pickets stood in front of a vehicle in order to prevent it from entering the employer's premises (*Broome v DPP* (1974)) and walked in a continuous circle at a factory entrance (*Tynan v Balmer* (1967)).

Public nuisance

This offence derives from common law and is committed where members of the public are obstructed in the exercise of rights which are common to all Her Majesty's subjects, including the right of free passage along the public highway. As with the more frequently charged offence under the Highways Act, it is necessary for the prosecution to prove unreasonable user.

Where an individual suffers special damage over and above that suffered by the rest of the public, an action in tort for public nuisance may also be brought: see *News Group Newspapers Ltd v Society of Graphical and Allied Trades* (1986).

Conspiracy and Protection of Property Act 1875

This Victorian statute made the following acts criminal if they are done 'wrongfully and without legal authority', with a view to compelling any person to do or abstain from doing any act which that person has a legal right to do:

- using violence or intimidating that person or his wife or children or injuring his property;
- persistently following that person about from place to place;
- hiding any tools, clothes or other property owned or used by such other person, or depriving him or hindering him in the use thereof;
- watching or besetting his house, residence or place of work, or the approach to such house, residence or place, or wherever the person happens to be;
- following such a person with two or more other persons, in a disorderly manner, in or through any street or road (see, now, s 241 of TULR(C)A 1992).

This provision was frequently resorted to during the miners' strike of 1984–85. Subsequently the Public Order Act 1986 increased the maximum penalty from three months' imprisonment and a £100 fine to six months' imprisonment and a fine (currently £5,000). The Act also made breach of what is now s 241 an arrestable offence.

One final point on this section concerns the question of whether mass picketing amounts to intimidation. In *Thomas v NUM (South Wales Area)* (1985), Scott J was of the view that not only was mass picketing a common law nuisance, but also that it amounted to intimidation under what is now s 241, even where there was no physical obstruction of those going to work.

Public Order Act 1986

Part I of the Public Order Act contained five new statutory offences which may be of relevance in the context of picketing. Sections 1–3 of the Act contain the offences of rioting, violent disorder and affray and replace the common law offences of riot, rout, unlawful assembly and affray, whose ambit was confused and uncertain. Sections 4 and 5 contain the more minor offences of causing fear or provocation of violence and causing harassment, alarm or distress.

Part II gives the police certain powers to impose conditions upon public processions and assemblies, in addition to their common law powers to take such action as may be necessary to prevent a breach of the peace.

Conclusion

The 1998 White Paper, *Fairness at Work*, contained a foreword by the Prime Minister, Tony Blair, in which he stated: 'There will be no going back. The days of strikes without ballots, mass picketing, closed shops and secondary action are over.' It remains to be seen whether, as he wished, no more employment legislation will pass through the current Parliament.